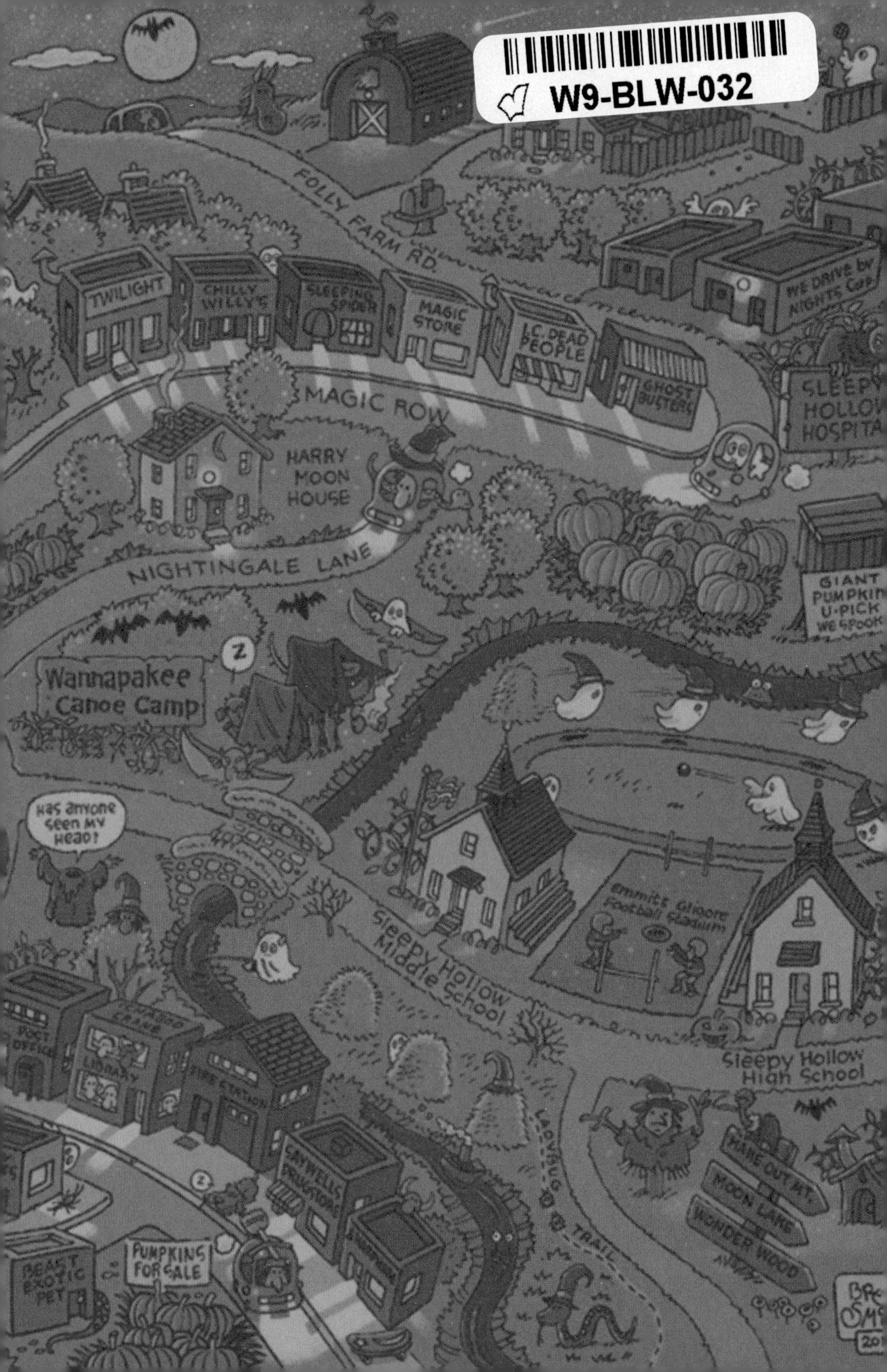
FOLLY FARM RD.
TWILIGHT
CHILLY WILLY'S
SLEEPING SPIDER
MAGIC STORE
I.C. DEAD PEOPLE
GHOST BUSTERS
MAGIC ROW
HARRY MOON HOUSE
NIGHTINGALE LANE
Wannapakee Canoe Camp
Has anyone seen my head?
Sleepy Hollow Middle School
Emmitt Gloore Football Stadium
Sleepy Hollow High School
POST OFFICE
LIBRARY
FIRE STATION
PUMPKINS FOR SALE
BEAST EXOTIC PET
TRAIL
HARE OUT MT.
MOON LAKE
WONDER WOOD

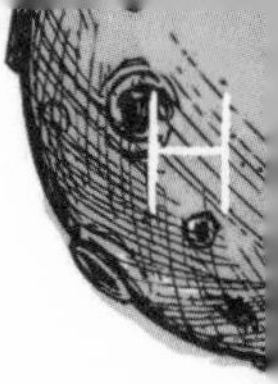

"Come home, Harry."

~ *Rabbit*

THE AMAZING ADVENTURES OF

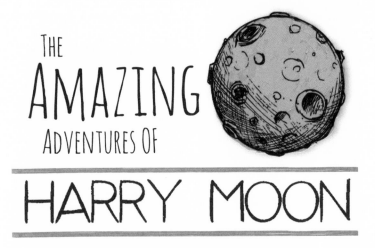

HARRY MOON

RUN, HARRY, RUN

by

Mark Andrew Poe

with Barry Napier

Illustrations by Christina Weidman

rabbit publishers

Run, Harry, Run (The Amazing Adventures of Harry Moon)
by Mark Andrew Poe
with Barry Napier

Rabbit Publishers
1624 W. Northwest Highway
Arlington Heights, IL 60004

Illustrations by Christina Weidman
Interior Design by Lewis Design & Marketing
Creative Consultants: David Kirkpatrick, Thom Black, and Paul Lewis

ISBN: 978-1-943785-42-1

10 9 8 7 6 5 4 3 2 1

1. Fiction - Action and Adventure 2. Children's Fiction
First Edition
Printed in U.S.A.

TABLE OF CONTENTS

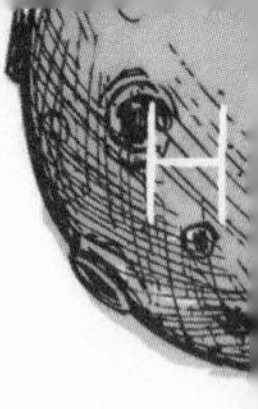

PROLOGUE

Halloween visited the little town of Sleepy Hollow and never left.

Many moons ago, a sly and evil mayor found the powers of darkness helpful in building Sleepy Hollow into "Spooky Town," one of the country's most celebrated attractions. Now, years later, a young eighth grade magician, Harry Moon, is chosen by the powers of light to do battle against the mayor and his evil consorts.

Welcome to *The Amazing Adventures of Harry Moon*. Darkness may have found a home in Sleepy Hollow, but if young Harry has anything to say about it, darkness will not be staying.

FAMILY, FRIENDS & FOES

Harry Moon

Harry is the thirteen-year-old hero of Sleepy Hollow. He is a gifted magician who is learning to use his abilities and understand what it means to possess the real magic.

An unlikely hero, Harry is shorter than his classmates and has a shock of inky, black hair. He loves his family and his town. Along with his friend Rabbit, Harry is determined to bring Sleepy Hollow back to its true and wholesome glory.

Rabbit

Now you see him. Now you don't. Rabbit is Harry Moon's friend. Some see him. Most can't.

Rabbit is a large, black-and-white, lop-eared, Harlequin rabbit. As Harry has discovered, having a friend like Rabbit has its consequences. Never stingy with advice and counsel, Rabbit always has Harry's back as Harry battles the evil that has overtaken Sleepy Hollow.

Mary Moon

Strong, fair, and spiritual, Mary Moon is Harry and Honey's mother. She is also mother to two-year-old Harvest. Mary is married to John Moon.

Mary is learning to understand Harry and his destiny. So far, she is doing a good job letting Harry and Honey fight life's battles. She's grateful that Rabbit has come alongside to support and counsel her. But like all moms, Mary often finds it difficult to let her children walk their own paths. Mary is a nurse at Sleepy Hollow Hospital.

IV

John Moon

John is the dad. He's a bit of a nerd. He works as an IT professional, and sometimes he thinks he would love it if his children followed in his footsteps. But he respects that Harry, Honey, and possibly Harvest will need to go their own way. John owns a classic sports car he calls Emma.

Titus Kligore

Titus is the mayor's son. He is a bully of the first degree but also quite conflicted when it comes to Harry. The two have managed to forge a tentative friendship, although Titus will

Honey Moon

She's a ten-year-old, sassy spitfire. And she's Harry's little sister. Honey likes to say she goes where she is needed, and sometimes this takes her into the path of danger.

Honey never gives in and never gives up when it comes to righting a wrong. Honey always looks out for her friends. Honey does not like that her town has been plunged into a state of eternal Halloween and is even afraid of the evil she feels lurking all around. But if Honey has anything to say about it, evil will not be sticking around.

III

Samson Dupree

Samson is the enigmatic owner of the Sleepy Hollow Magic Shoppe. He is Harry's mentor and friend. When needed, Samson teaches Harry new tricks and helps him understand his gift of magic.

Samson arranged for Rabbit to become Harry's sidekick and friend. Samson is a timeless, eccentric man who wears purple robes, red slippers, and a gold crown. Sometimes, Samson shows up in mysterious ways. He even appeared to Harry's mother shortly after Harry's birth.

assert his bully strength on Harry from time to time.

Titus is big. He towers over Harry. But in a kind of David vs. Goliath way, Harry has learned which tools are best to counteract Titus's assaults while most of the Sleepy Hollow kids fear him. Titus would probably rather not be a bully, but with a dad like Maximus Kligore, he feels trapped in the role.

Maximus Kligore

The epitome of evil, nastiness, and greed, Maximus Kligore is the mayor of Sleepy Hollow. To bring in the cash, Maximus turned the town into the nightmarish, Halloween attraction it is today.

He commissions the evil-tinged celebrations in town. Maximus is planning to take Sleepy Hollow with him to Hell. But will he? He knows Harry Moon is a threat to his dastardly ways, but try as he might, he has yet to rid himself of Harry's meddling.

Kligore lives on Folly Farm and owns most of the town, including the town newspaper.

A MISSING MOON

Sleepy Hollow was usually a very quiet town at night. Anyone out walking the streets once the moon came up would be treated to a peaceful little town where anything was possible. The only sounds this person might hear would be the random hooting of an owl, the chirping of crickets, and maybe the groaning noises from the wind passing through the branches of trees in the cemetery. A few years back, a kid named

Barry Beetle swore he heard a very large splashing noise coming from Scarlet Letter Lake around midnight—large enough to be a whale or maybe even a kraken. But those rumors were passed off as Barry Beetle's imagination and tendency to lie.

For the most part, Sleepy Hollow was quiet when it got dark. That, of course, didn't mean that nothing ever happened in the tiny, little town when the sun went down.

Listen close enough and you'll hear the clock tower ticking in the center of Town Square. Or maybe you'll hear the scurrying of millions of little legs as insects pass across Ladybug Trail. If you're really unfortunate, you might even hear the night winds passing between the legs of the Headless Horseman statue in Town Square, a noise that some say sounds like screaming children.

One sound no one ever expects to hear in Sleepy Hollow is the sound of weeping. Sure, there might be the silent crying of a teenager with a broken heart from time to time, but never an open and loud wailing.

Tonight, however, was the exception.

Anyone that happened to be walking down Nightingale Lane tonight would hear the very noticeable crying of a woman. The noise was coming from the Moon residence, particularly from the heart and mouth of Mary Moon.

Outside of the Moon house, a few people were gathered in support. Some burned candles in a sort of lazy vigil while others were visibly praying. They all looked toward the Moon household, concerned about Mary Moon and the reason she was crying.

Within the Moon home, every light was on . . . all except for one. The one room that remained in darkness belonged to Harry Moon. Harry was a bright and unique young man, a thirteen-year-old that was known throughout Sleepy Hollow as having a talent for magic. Quiet, yet very active, Harry was liked by most and seen as a promising and rather special boy.

A few of the people on the Moons' lawn looked to that darkened window and frowned. One of Harry's best friends, Declan Dickinson, regarded the darkened window with an intense sense of loss.

Declan had not seen Harry all day—not since meeting up with him before school that morning. This was strange, as Declan saw Harry *all the time*. Before school, in school, and after school. But not today.

In fact, *no one* had seen Harry Moon all day. From what the Sleepy Hollow police could figure out, he had gone missing sometime in the morning. As soon as this news got out, it had spread through Sleepy Hollow, and now, less than sixteen hours after he had woken up that morning, the town was concerned about Harry Moon.

No one had any leads . . . no clues or ideas of where Harry had gone.

So for now, all Declan and the other concerned citizens of Sleepy Hollow could do was show their support in meager candlelight vigils and stand by while Mary Moon and the rest of the Moon family waited inside, hoping someone would soon find Harry.

But until then, a sad series of sobs filled the night, coming from the Moon home like the wails of a ghost as everyone waited for Harry Moon to come home.

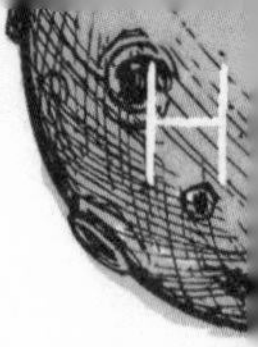
H

19 Hours Earlier

arry Moon had an alarm clock that was topped with a figurine of Elvis Gold, his favorite magician. Every morning, the Elvis Gold alarm clock would blare its alarm—Elvis Gold repeatedly chanting *"Presto!"* and *"Abracadabra!"* It never failed to get Harry out of bed with a spring in his step and a smile on his face.

This morning, though, the Elvis Gold alarm clock did not wake Harry up. Instead, the

1

vibrating of his cell phone from beside the alarm clock stirred him awake. Still half-asleep and blurry-eyed, Harry squinted at the clock as his cell phone continued to vibrate. The clock read 6:32— a whole twenty-eight minutes before Elvis Gold's tinny voice usually woke him.

He picked up his phone and saw he had received a text from a number he wasn't familiar with. The text message was simple but also sounded exciting. It read:

> Care to Join a New Mobile Game for Magicians Only? Respond back with YES or NO if you want to play MagiKwest!

Although he was still rather tired, the message was very enticing. There were no games out there for aspiring magicians. The thought of a game geared specifically to his interests was exciting. Without giving it much thought, Harry responded with

> YES.

He stumbled out of bed and threw on his clothes for the day. As he was about to head out of his bedroom to brush his teeth, his phone vibrated behind him again. He picked it up once more and saw another message from the same unfamiliar number. The new message read:

> Welcome to MagiKwest! The only mobile game for great, young magicians! Please understand that your name was provided to us through people that know about your talents and care greatly about you! However, your involvement with MagiKwest must remain a secret! To experience the fun and adventure of the game, you must tell no one that you are playing. If you can agree to these terms, we can begin! Please respond with YES or NO.

9

"This is so cool," Harry thought, as he quickly typed in

> YES.

Now more excited than ever, he rushed to the bathroom and brushed his teeth. He then ran through his usual weekday morning routine of eating breakfast quickly with his family and then heading out the door to meet with up Hao, Declan, and Bailey a few blocks away. If he was quick and not distracted, it could all be done in less than twenty minutes. And with the new excitement about MagiKwest in his head, he was moving quicker than normal.

As he sat down at the kitchen table with his bowl of cereal and cheese toast, he felt his phone vibrate in his pocket. He wanted to check it then and there, but his family was bustling around the kitchen. Honey, his younger sister, and Harvest, his younger brother, were both at the table with him. Honey was eating a bagel, and Harvest seemed to be mashing his cereal into tiny crumbs that he wet with his milk, turning it into a paste before he ate it.

Harry grimaced and quickly ate his own cereal. As he did, Mary Moon came into the kitchen. She was carrying her usual mug of morning coffee when she sat down. She stared across the table at Harry and smiled curiously.

"You're eating awfully fast," she said.

Harry shrugged and said, "I guess I'm just really hungry."

"Hungry," Harvest mimicked. He smeared more of his cereal paste across his mouth and grinned. "Hungry!"

11

"Big day at school today for you guys?" Mary asked. Behind her, John Moon was pouring his own coffee, in a rush as usual.

"Same as always," Harry said, feeling an intense urge to leave the room so he could check the text message waiting for him in his pocket.

"Not for me," Honey complained. "I have a stupid spelling test. Stupid. S-T-U-P-I-D."

"You've studied for it, though," John Moon said. "You'll nail it. I know you will."

"I hope so," Honey said, nervously.

Harry barely heard the conversation. He was too preoccupied with trying to imagine what a mobile game geared toward young magicians might look like.

He finished up his cereal, placed the empty

12

bowl in the kitchen sink, and then hugged his parents goodbye. His dad gave him the usual hair ruffle, while his mother gave him her patented almost-sloppy kiss on the forehead.

"Have a great day, sweetie," Mary Moon said.

"Thanks," Harry said, already hurrying for the door. He managed to keep his cool until he was standing outside in the morning sun, not wanting his parents—or especially Honey —to think that he was up to something. He hated to keep *anything* from his folks, but the rules of the MagiKwest game had clearly said to tell no one about it if he wanted to get the full effects.

13

Harry walked quickly to the end of the block before he pulled his phone out of his pocket. The text message that awaited him provided a link and a simple welcome.

> To get started, click the link and download the game. Your first task is waiting!

Harry wasted no time, clicking the link right away. It took him to a simple mobile site that had only a single download button and another welcoming message. It read:

> You're just ONE CLICK AWAY from enjoying the only game for young magicians! Download now and start your quest to discover how to reach your true magical abilities!

14

Smiling widely, Harry tapped the download button. A little spinning wheel popped up on his screen, and within ten seconds, the MagiKwest app was downloaded and added to his phone. Harry opened the app right away, walking slowly down the street with his face glued to the screen.

The app was quite simple. A little, animated magic hat popped up on the screen. A word balloon came out of its mouth and said:

> To begin, please enter your name!

Harry typed his name in with the little

keyboard that the app provided. Right away, another word balloon popped up. This one said:

> Welcome, Harry! The Key to Everything awaits you in the Sleepy Hollow Bell Tower! You have only one hour to complete this task! Run, Harry, run!

Beside the little cartoon hat, a timer popped up. It started at one hour and then turned to 59:59, counting down the seconds.

15

Harry frowned as he read over the message again. How was he supposed to find a key in the Bell Tower in the next hour? He had to get to school. He wondered if the task would *really* no longer be available if he waited until the afternoon. He hated to think that he had finally found this awesome game and might not be able to play it because of the weird time limits it seemed to place on the tasks.

Harry then looked at the small clock in the upper right hand corner of his phone. It read 7:32. That gave him exactly forty-three minutes to get to school. He usually got there about ten minutes before the bell rang to start classes, mainly to hang with Hao, Bailey, and Declan, his best friends and members of the Good Mischief Team. He could skip getting there early for *one* day. It wouldn't hurt anything.

He figured it would take him fifteen minutes to get to the Bell Tower and then another fifteen minutes to get from the Bell Tower to school. That gave him almost another full fifteen minutes to find the key.

If there's a key at all, Harry thought to himself. *What sort of game can really hide things in the user's town? That's impossible . . . isn't it?*

He wasn't sure. He knew that there was some new game that used what was known as "augmented reality" to hunt down imaginary monsters in your own back yard. So maybe the set-up of MagiKwest wasn't entirely impossible.

"Oh, what the heck?" Harry said, making the decision right then and there.

Still, he had to meet with the guys. If he didn't show up, they would worry. Whenever one of them was sick and wasn't going to make it to school the next day, they always called one another. He hated to do it . . . but he was going to have to lie to his friends. Sticking to the MagiKwest rules, *no one* could know about it. Not even the Good Mischief Team.

He did his best to look sad and weak as he made his way down the street. He looked up ahead and saw his friends waiting for him at the end of the next street. One of them—Declan, he thought—gave an exaggerated wave. Harry waved back, a slow wave that he hoped looked tired and weak.

Harry's heart felt like it was sagging in his chest when he reached them. Was he really going to do this? Was he really going to lie to his best friends like this? A very big part of him wanted to share the news about MagiKwest. After all, it was an awesome app, and he felt like he had to tell *someone*.

But the fear of losing access to the game won out as he approached the rest of the Good Mischief Team. When he drew up next to them, he gave them a small smile and made sure to have his eyes flutter and sag a bit. Apparently, it worked better than he could have imagined.

"Yikes, Harry," Hao said. "Are you okay?'

Harry shrugged. "I don't know. I'm not feeling so great."

"What's up?" Bailey asked.

"My stomach is feeling weird and I . . . I don't know. I just feel sort of yucky. Like really tired and lazy."

Bailey made a show of stepping back and covering his nose and mouth. "Well, I don't want to catch it!"

"For real," Declan said. "Maybe you should go back home."

Harry pretended to think this over. In the back

18

of his head, he was also trying to figure out how faking being sick might get him in even more trouble. But he figured he could worry about that when the time came.

"Yeah, I think I will," Harry said. "Thanks, guys."

"Don't thank us," Bailey said, smiling. "Just stay away!"

They all laughed good-naturedly as Harry gave a pitiful little wave and turned away from his friends. He felt very bad—he nearly *did* feel sick for lying to them.

He made it to the end of the street before he dared to look back over his shoulder. He could barely see the guys now, shrinking into the distance as they made their way to school. Quickly, Harry dashed to the left, crossing the street and heading off in the opposite direction.

He headed back down Nightingale Lane and cut over toward Magic Row. The Bell Tower was there, the original foundation for what was now Sleepy Hollow Town Hall. The Bell Tower sat high above Town Hall's roof and as far as Harry knew, had never been used—not in his lifetime, anyway.

As he got closer to Magic Row with his book bag slung over his shoulder, Harry realized that this might be the first time in his life that he had kept a secret—from his parents and his friends. But it was just a game . . . so there was no real harm in it.

Right?

It certainly felt like it was harmless as he reached Magic Row and saw the Bell Tower looming over the buildings. Anything *this* exciting couldn't be *bad*, could it?

It was not something Harry was too concerned with at that moment. With the little timer on the MagiKwest app now at 45:07, Harry kept his eyes locked on the Bell Tower, pushing any thoughts of his family, friends, and school out of his head.

THE KEY
TO EVERYTHING

I t occurred to Harry as he reached Town Hall that he had never actually been inside the building. That's why he had no idea the place didn't open its doors until nine in the morning. He looked at the closed doors, wondering if there was another way in. As he looked around, he noticed that the morning traffic in town was starting to pick up. If he didn't hurry up, someone that knew his folks would see him, and it might raise questions later.

Harry looked up at the Bell Tower and had a thought. Because it was the original foundation for Town Hall, he knew that the actual building that housed the tower and the dead bell inside was located behind Town Hall. Maybe there was a way in somewhere along the back of the Town Hall building.

22

He sprinted around the side of Town Hall, amused that this was one part of town he had never taken the time to see. Town Hall came to an end in the back with a simple set of concrete steps that were attached to the Bell Tower with a very small sidewalk. The two buildings were attached by a set of iron handrails. Harry followed these rails to an open archway that led into the structure of the Bell Tower. It was open, like a big gazebo almost, except for the rear wall; there, a set of old, wooden stairs led straight up.

Harry dashed to the stairs, a little creeped

out by the way they groaned under his weight. He followed the stairs up until he was no longer in the open air beneath the structure of the Bell Tower. He was now inside the building, climbing up a rather narrow set of stairs that went straight up without any means of getting off of them until the top of the stairs. Dust and grime were everywhere. He found himself swatting at thick cobwebs as he finally reached the top of the stairs and came to a big, open space.

23

The bell hung from the top of the triangle-shaped ceiling. It hung down so low that it nearly touched the scarred, wooden floor. Harry ran his hand along it, amazed by how old it seemed. For a second or two, he nearly forgot why he was there in the first place.

He looked back down to his phone and saw the same screen. The little magic hat still said

The Key to Every-thing awaits you in the Sleepy Hollow Bell Tower!

Beside it, the timer was down to 36:46.

Harry pocketed the phone and started to look around the top of the Bell Tower. If he was going to get to school on time, he'd have to find the key in less than twenty minutes. He looked at the floor and saw that there were some large spaces between the floorboards—not too big but certainly large enough to slide a key into if it were sitting up on its side. Within a few minutes of searching, though, it became clear that the key was not hiding in the floor.

24

He then looked at the bell. It was huge and bronze-colored, easily as wide as two Harrys placed side by side. When he approached it, he could smell its rust and old age. He dropped down to the floor again and slid up under it. He knew it was probably dangerous. Lord only knew how long the ancient bell had been hanging there from the old, decrepit rope system that held it in place within the tower. He figured he had better be quick.

As his body pushed dust bunnies and years of dirt to the side, Harry slid under the open mouth along the bottom of the bell. When he looked up, there was nothing but blackness. He could barely see the clapper hanging from the top of the bell, frozen and useless for several years.

25

But then he saw something else too . . . a slight flicker of dull light to his left and a few inches over his head. Harry reached up into the darkness inside the bell and touched the weird light.

Only, it wasn't a light at all.

It was a key. It had been taped to the inside of the bell.

He carefully peeled the tape away. It was sticky and seemed to be untouched by the dust inside of the bell. Harry was pretty sure it had been placed there very recently. As the tape peeled away, the key fell directly into Harry's open palm. Harry slid out from beneath the bell and looked curiously at the key as he dusted the dirt from his back and bottom.

It looked like every other key he had ever seen. At first glance, there seemed to be absolutely nothing special about it at all. The only thing unique about it was a number that had been professionally engraved into the head of it. That number was 206.

Confused and a little disappointed, Harry got to his feet and brushed the dust off of his clothes. He eyed the key again before pocketing it and gathering up his book bag. When it was on his shoulders, he checked the time and saw that he had twenty minutes before school started—just enough time to get there without having to rush.

Harry headed back down the winding stairs that led to the bottom of the bell tower. The morning air was cool on his skin, making him realize just how hot and stuffy it had been in the top of the bell tower. He started down Main Street, already wondering if this so-called MagiKwest was some sort of scam when his phone buzzed from his pocket.

He took it out and saw that he had a notification from the MagiKwest app. Still walking down the street, Harry pulled up the app and saw that he had a message. It read:

27

> Congratulations on completing your first task! Now that you have the key, ask yourself … why would there be a number on the key? Where in town would you need a key to get into something other than a house? You have 30 minutes to discover your next clue! Run, Harry, run!

Harry stopped walking and re-read the message. He wasn't sure if it was supposed to be some sort of subtle riddle or just a weird question. Whatever it was, it had him thinking. He put his phone in his pocket and again looked at the key. If the key wasn't to a house, what else could it possibly unlock? What else in Sleepy Hollow had numbers on it that could be locked and unlocked?

He re-examined the key and saw that it was a little bit smaller than a typical house key. He wondered if it was to a safe in the bank or maybe to a—

"That's it," Harry muttered to himself.

He was pretty sure he knew where to go, but there was no way he could get the next clue *and* get to school on time. And even if he could manage to get it done, there was no telling what sort of time limit he'd have to find the next clue. But . . . this was just a game. What was the worst that could happen if he didn't find a clue in the time it gave him? However fun and mysterious the game might be, it wasn't worth missing school and getting in trouble.

Was it?

Standing there in the middle of Main Street, Harry sensed that he had a very important and nearly adult-like decision to make. He could be responsible and forget the game; he could go straight to school and do the right thing. Or he could run the risk of being late so he could follow up on this next clue.

29

The decision did not take long to make. With a mischievous smile, Harry pulled out his phone again and, rather than head to Sleepy Hollow Middle School, started off toward the Sleepy Hollow Post Office.

30

Mr. Preston Fang

When Harry got to the post office, it was 8:03. He knew this meant he'd definitely be late, and although this made him feel guilty, there was an odd sort of excitement to it as well. Harry was not the type of boy that got into trouble. He'd never been grounded, although he did get a little rambunctious from time to time. Still, intentionally running late for school was a whole new sort of adventure.

As Harry walked into the post office, he noticed that a few people on the street and coming out of the post office looked at him a little suspiciously. He wondered if any of them knew his parents and if they might mention seeing him scrambling nervously into the post office when he should have been headed to school. With that thought spooking him, Harry lowered his head and squeezed into the post office as an older man came out.

Inside the post office, the smell of paper was thick in the air. He'd been in the Sleepy Hollow Post Office a few times with his mom so knew the layout well. To the right of the teller window, where a cheerful old man helped people with stamps and packages, there was a wall of post office boxes. These, Harry knew, were for people that lived in places that did not have mailboxes and got their mail sent directly to the post office. Each of the boxes was made of metal. Each one featured a number and a small lock on its face.

Harry walked quickly to the post office boxes, grateful that no one was standing by them. He felt like there was electricity passing through his body as he reached into his pocket and withdrew the key he'd retrieved from the Bell Tower. He found Box 206 and tried the key. There was a moment when Harry was sure this was too easy—sure that the key would not fit and that he had been wrong in his guess.

But the key slid in easily. When Harry turned it, the lock inside made a delightful clicking sound as it opened. Harry pulled open the small metal door and peered inside. Numerous letters and newspapers and fliers were stuffed inside, so thick that Harry was amazed that the box hadn't started to bulge out at the sides.

In front of all of this mail was an index card with three words written on it: Deliver me, please.

Harry grabbed the index card and the pile of mail inside. The letter on top was from

33

someone in California and was addressed to a man named Preston Fang. The post office box belonged to Mr. Fang, and according to the envelope, he lived on Mayflower Road.

Harry glanced at his phone. The little countdown clock on the MagiKwest app was down to 19:30 and the current time was 8:07. Harry realized that if he continued to follow this trail of adventure that MagiKwest was setting out for him, he could be very late for school. For all he knew, it could keep him busy all day, and he'd end up missing the entire day.

Deep in his heart, he knew it was irresponsible, but he simply didn't care. This game seemed to be based on some sort of magic that he badly wanted to understand. The app had known when he'd retrieved the key, after all. More than that, someone had taken the time to hide the key at some point—and very recently, if the fresh sticky tape was any clue. Suddenly, it was starting to feel like much more than just some silly game.

It was simply all too much to ignore. He was

sure he'd get in trouble for skipping school, but whatever journey MagiKwest had him on suddenly seemed more than just plain old fun. Now it seemed very important in a way that Harry couldn't quite understand.

With a heavy but excited heart, Harry reached into the mailbox and gathered up all of Preston Fang's mail. Not wanting to seem more out of place than he actually was, Harry slid it all into his book bag. Seeing the books in there made him feel fear and guilt again, but it was gone as soon as he zipped the book bag closed.

35

Putting the key back into his pocket and holding his phone in his hand in the hopes that it might buzz soon, Harry left the post office and headed for Mayflower Road. He walked quickly, looking at the ground in the hopes that no one would recognize him. He knew that skipping school was wrong, but there was an adventure here . . . a mystery like he had never experienced before.

He could pay the consequences later and

hope his parents would extend some grace. For now, he was on a mission that would take its next step at 706 Mayflower Road, the home of Mr. Preston Fang.

Harry had never heard of Preston Fang, so he certainly had no idea who the man was. But when he arrived at 706 Mayflower Road, just seeing the house made Harry envision a certain sort of person. The overgrown grass, the weeds in the flower beds, and the dingy welcome mat on the porch made Harry think of a man that lived alone—probably an older man with white hair and a dry laugh.

Hefting his book bag over his shoulder, Harry approached the front door. He made a fist and hesitantly knocked on the front door. It was silly, but the sound made Harry jump a bit. He took a step back from the door and waited for it to be answered. He could hear someone moving around inside, a shuffling series of footsteps approaching the door.

It finally opened with a creaking noise, and Harry discovered that his hunch had been

correct. An older man stood there, looking down at Harry. Most of his hair was white, including the scruff on his cheeks and chin. He had bushy eyebrows, a large nose, and a very grumpy expression.

"Yeah?" the old man asked.

"Sorry to bother you, sir," Harry said. "But are you Mr. Fang? Preston Fang?"

The old man made a sort of huffing noise that might have been a murmur of agreement. "Aye, that's me."

"I . . . well, I was told to bring your mail to you," Harry said, slipping his book bag off of his shoulders and onto the porch.

Mr. Fang grinned for a moment and nodded. "Oh, is that so?"

"Yes, sir."

"And who asked you to deliver it?"

"Well, I don't know, exactly."

He handed Mr. Fang his jumble of mail. The moment the stack of mail exchanged hands, Harry felt his phone buzz inside his pocket. He withdrew it and saw another notification from MagiKwest. He checked it as Mr. Fang looked through the stack of mail with something closer to anger than interest.

On the screen, a new message from

MagiKwest read:

> Another task completed! Stand by for your next instruction, to be given to you by Mr. Fang!

Harry was very confused now. And, for the first time since waking up to the text from MagiKwest, a bit scared. How could a mobile game *possibly* know that he'd already delivered the mail? More than that, how was Mr. Fang involved? Was he behind the game or was he an unknowing part of someone else's strategy?

The worst thing of all was that Harry could not ask Mr. Fang because the instructions had told him to tell no one that he was playing.

Mr. Fang was looking at him now, his eyes staring hard from underneath his bushy, white eyebrows. "Say, what's your name?" Mr. Fang asked.

"Harry. Harry Moon."

Again, the old man offered a smile. "That's an interesting name. You must catch ribbing from your classmates at school, eh?"

"Sometimes," Harry said, embarrassed. Thinking of his schoolmates—particularly Hao, Bailey, and Declan—Harry felt another pang of guilt. School would have started by now and here he was, on a strange old man's porch because some mysterious mobile game had sent him here.

"Well, kids can be mean sometimes," Mr. Fang said.

"Can I ask why I was asked to deliver your mail?"

"I have no idea. I was told a while ago to never worry about it. The mayor knows I don't like going out during the day. He takes care of me. I have a condition, you see . . . the sun . . . "

"Oh," Harry said. "The mayor . . . "

"Yeah, he's a character alright," Mr. Fang said,

sensing Harry's unease. "But he knows about my condition. And he's helped me. My ... *ailment* doesn't allow for me to travel much. When the sun goes down I get . . . a little different."

"Different how?"

"Ah, that's nothing you want to hear about. Let's just say I steer away from garlic and mirrors. And steaks."

"Like wooden stakes?"

41

"No, like filet mignons and rib eyes. They gross us out, too."

"Us?" Harry squeaked. "Are you . . . ?"

"Please don't even say the word," Mr. Fang said, irritated. "It's so boring and generic. Ever since people started writing stories where we sparkle and fall in love, we've become something of a joke." He made a chuffing sound here, clearly mad about something that Harry didn't quite understand. "I should be sleeping in a coffin right now, right? There's a lot that fairy tales and myths get wrong."

Harry started taking a step back, ready to bolt. If Mr. Fang was what Harry thought he was . . . well, that was sort of scary and out of Harry's comfort zone.

"Ah, listen to me yammering on," Mr. Fang said. "I was told that the next person to deliver my mail would want a little something from me. A clue of some kind, perhaps?"

"Yes, sir," Harry replied.

"Well, let me just say this: this sun in the morning sky is dangerous for me. I think there might be relief for both of us on Henry David Thoreau's backside."

Harry stood there, waiting for clarification, for several seconds. But the only other thing he got was another of Mr. Fang's sly, crooked smiles. The old man then nodded to Harry and closed his door, leaving him alone on the front porch.

"That's it?" Harry asked the door.

He turned away from the door and walked back out onto Mr. Fang's overgrown lawn. Again, his phone started buzzing in his pocket. Harry found another message waiting for him from MagiKwest. This one was more to the point and basic than the other ones. This one simply read:

One hour to complete this task. Run, Harry, run!

43

Beside the message, the countdown clock popped up again and started to count down his hour.

Absolutely baffled by Mr. Fang's final comments, Harry walked slowly down Mayflower Road. There was no traffic venturing down the quiet little street, so there was no real risk of being seen. He checked his clock and saw that it was now 8:55. He was over half an hour late for school. If he went now, he could maybe explain to his teacher that he'd simply slept in and—

But that *would* be a lie, Harry thought.

A little upset with himself, Harry knew there was no turning back. He *had* to keep going. He *had* to figure out what was at the end of MagiKwest and why he had been selected to play in the first place.

That's when Harry Moon accepted the fact that he'd be skipping school today. Rather than sitting in homeroom with his friends, Harry Moon finished out the eight o' clock hour of that morning walking alone down Mayflower Road, thinking about Henry David Thoreau's backside.

SAFELY AMONG THE DEAD

arry spent the next fifteen minutes walking up and down Mayflower Road, trying to figure out Mr. Fang's cryptic and humorous closing comment. He didn't dare venture onto Main Street or Magic Row. Those were the busier roads in town, and he knew that he'd be busted for sure if he was spotted there on a weekday morning while all other kids were in school.

The name of Henry David Thoreau was familiar. One of the things Sleepy Hollow was known for—aside from the almost iconic statue of the Headless Horseman in the town square— was the surprising number of dead authors. There were several of them buried in the Sleepy Hollow Cemetery. Harry was pretty sure that Henry David Thoreau was one of them. Still, even if that was the case, what did Thoreau's backside have to do with anything?

Harry wasn't sure, but he did know one thing: the countdown timer on the MagiKwest app was now down to 44:39. And since the only immediate connection Harry could make was to Henry David Thoreau's grave, he figured he might as well start in the Sleepy Hollow Cemetery. Fortunately, he could take Mayflower Road most of the way there. He'd go past a few small fields, and then hopefully, he'd be able to sneak through the woods, avoiding Main Street altogether, to reach the outer edge of the cemetery.

By the time Harry had reached the place where he'd have to step off of Mayflower Road and through a small field toward the woods, his sense of adventure was almost completely driving him. He had never done anything this secretive—this *risky*. As he walked into the small field to the east of Mayflower Road and headed for the forest beyond, there was a small part of him that was actually excited about the idea of getting in trouble. This was a very uncharacteristic feeling for Harry, but he was far too pumped to notice or care.

He finally stepped into the forest and took a moment to get his bearings. The last thing he needed was to get turned around in the woods and end up on the other end of Mayflower Road or, even worse, miss the cemetery altogether and come out on Mt. Sinai Road. He took the time to look all around and was pretty sure that if he headed straight and slightly to the left, he'd reach the back gate of the cemetery fairly quickly. Sleepy Hollow wasn't exactly a booming

47

metropolis; it was very unlikely he'd actually get *lost* in the forest.

He walked in what he thought was the right direction, smiling as he wondered what sort of conversations Hao, Declan, and Bailey might be having. Did they think he was sick? Did they maybe think he had gotten into some mischief with his magic? Whatever the case, Harry was pretty sure that he would not get out of this without his parents finding out. There would be questions, and he'd likely get into trouble for his actions. But again, he figured he could worry about that when the time came. For now, there was a magical quest to complete.

Harry walked through the dark forest for roughly ten minutes before he saw the high iron posts of the cemetery fence. The branches of the trees over his head seemed to actually point him in that direction. With twigs and fallen leaves crunching underfoot, Harry dashed for the fence.

It was an old, rustic fence with posts that stood about twelve feet high. Decorative points

and edges adorned the top of the posts. Anyone that tried to climb over the posts would likely be impaled. But Harry was a very thin thirteen-year-old. He looked at the posts and the black iron slats that ran between them, fairly certain he could just slip through them. He removed his backpack and pushed it through the slats. He then sucked in a deep breath, drawing in his chest and stomach. He put one foot through the slats, the foot landing on the cemetery grounds on the other side. He kept his stomach sucked in and slid the rest of his body through. He barely fit; his nose brushed against the slat in front of him.

But when it was all said and done, he found himself standing along the back stretch of lawn in the Sleepy Hollow Cemetery. He glanced at his phone and saw that the MagiKwest countdown clock now read 31:02. He looked out at the graveyard, frowning at the countless headstones.

He had no idea where Henry David Thoreau's grave was but figured that it would be an older grave. Assuming this was a safe bet, Harry started walking among the rows of tombstones, looking for the older ones. As he did, he also pulled out his phone and ran a quick search for Thoreau.

Within seconds, he discovered that Henry David Thoreau, author of *Walden* and various poems, died in 1862. Harry also saw a picture of Thoreau's grave. The tombstone was a small one and, unlike most traditional grave markers, bore only his first name rather than his last.

With a clear image to go by, Harry started to walk faster. He came to a section of the graveyard where the dates started to dwindle down into the late 1800s. He continued scanning, very aware of the countdown clock still in his hand.

Within another few minutes, Harry came to a row of graves that were separated more than the others he had passed. There was more space between each tombstone, making it easy for him to spot the small, unremarkable one near the end of the row. Harry dashed to it and saw right away that it was the one he was looking for. A few dead flowers lay scattered around the base. In the center of the stone was the name *HENRY.*

51

Harry stared at the grave for a moment, trying to be respectful by not simply observing up close. Someone had been laid to rest here. While he was excited and even looking forward to the chance to get in trouble, Harry also knew that respecting the dead was a simple matter of good manners.

Henry David Thoreau's backside . . . Harry thought. *What does that even mean?*

A terrible image occurred to Harry—a vision of having to get a shovel and go digging to get a peek at Henry David Thoreau's backside. *Yuck . . .*

Harry started to slowly circle the grave, looking for any other clues. As he did, a sudden realization hit him like a hurled rock right between the eyes. Maybe it wasn't Thoreau's backside he was looking for. Maybe it was the *grave's* backside.

Harry went to the back of the headstone and smiled. There, at the very bottom of the stone where it met with the ground, was what looked like a tiny keyhole. Frowning, Harry ran his hand along the keyhole, wondering if there was another key somewhere.

He took the key to Mr. Fang's post office box out of his pocket and tried it. The key was too big for the keyhole and simply clinked against the old stone. Harry backed away for a moment, trying to figure out where he had gone wrong. While thinking, he looked back at his phone. The MagiKwest clock now read 26:15.

He had a keyhole with a key that didn't fit. And unless he had missed an obvious clue somewhere, he had no more information to go on. So maybe he was just overlooking something very simple . . .

"Wait a minute," Harry said to himself.

53

This was an app for aspiring magicians. So maybe that meant a little magic could help. Sure. Why not? It was certainly worth a shot. Harry dug into his book bag and took out his magic wand. Holding it in the middle of a cemetery felt a little spooky, but it was familiar to his hand, and the feel of it calmed him down. He set Mr. Fang's key down on top of the headstone and pointed the wand at it. With great concentration, Harry waved the wand and said,

"ABRACADABRA!"

The key leaped several feet in the air, giving off a chiming noise as it rocketed off of the stone. It then turned in the air and fell to the ground in front of Harry's feet. Harry bent over to pick it up and saw that the post office box key was no longer silver and basic. It was now made of copper with a very long body and a head that looked very much like an old-fashioned skeleton key.

Harry placed his wand back into his bag and approached the back of Thoreau's grave. He inserted the new key into the little keyhole and found that it fit perfectly. With sweaty palms and a thrumming heart, Harry turned the key.

Something inside the old headstone rumbled and clicked. Harry felt the ground shifting slightly under his feet. Before Harry had time to truly get frightened, a small compartment along the back of the tombstone fell open. A small piece of rolled up parchment fell out of the compartment.

Harry picked the paper up and unrolled it. The paper was yellowed with age and crumbled apart at the edges. He wondered just how long it had been in hiding. On the paper, a short poem was written, along with a series of what looked to be random numbers. Harry read it all, trying to make sense of it.

> *The mayor's home, a sordid place*
> *And yet, a beautiful walnut tree.*
> *Beneath it all, a large stone face*
> *with eyes that cannot see.*
> *5 6 1 9 9 4*

As Harry read over the paper for the second time, his phone buzzed, letting him know that he had received a notification. He pulled it out and saw another message from MagiKwest. It read:

> Outstanding! By discovering this clue, you have truly proven yourself as a great magician! Now it gets harder. Are you ready? You have one hour to complete the next task. Run, Harry, run!

"What next task?" Harry asked, his voice

55

alone in the cemetery giving him the creeps. As far as he knew, there was no task to complete.

He read the poem again, pretty sure he knew what he was supposed to do but feeling like he might be taking things too far. *The mayor's home*, Harry thought. *That's Folly Farm.*

Harry slung his book bag onto his shoulder. He checked the time and saw that it was 9:40. He thought the streets would be a little clearer now, as most people were at work or school. Folly Farm was on the other side of town—a twenty-minute walk at least—but that was the least of his worries.

Harry and Mayor Kligore were arch enemies. And if the mayor caught sight of Harry on his property, there could be a whole new level of trouble for Harry to deal with.

But the MagiKwest countdown clock was ticking. He'd already wasted two minutes standing in the graveyard trying to sort through everything. And since he'd already crossed the line by skipping school, why stop now?

    With a heavy sigh and the stirring of nervousness in his stomach, Harry headed to the graveyard's iron fence and slipped back out into the woods. He started walking out toward Mayflower Road, heading straight for enemy territory.

58

THE WALNUT TREE

olly Farm sat on what was nearly the outskirts of town, situated on a hill that overlooked Sleepy Hollow. Harry always thought this was so the often-evil Mayor Kligore could keep an eye on the town's residents. Harry had been to the farm on a few occasions, and it had always ended in an epic confrontation of some kind.

When the farm came into view—the large, white house and the sheds and barns that set on the property behind it—Harry reached into his book bag and withdrew his wand. He then checked the MagiKwest countdown clock and saw that it had taken him a little more than twenty minutes to get across town. The clock currently read 38:17.

He paused at the top of the driveway and re-read the message he had found on the backside of Thoreau's grave. He figured he needed to take it one clue at a time. And after the mention of the mayor's home, there was mention of a walnut tree. Harry had no idea what a walnut tree looked like, but he *did* know what walnuts looked like. He also saw that there were none in the front yard. In fact, there were no trees in the front yard, as it was cleared off to showcase the elaborate landscaping and flowerbeds.

The idea of stepping foot on the mayor's

property was terrifying. Harry hoped the mayor was just like anyone else and worked out of an office in town. With a heavy sigh, Harry walked into the yard. He stayed to the side, planning to dash into the surrounding forest if anyone happened to come out of the house. With his eye on the house, Harry made his way around to the back yard where several trees covered most of the ground. He counted thirteen trees in the back yard, all of them stripped of their leaves. Since he could not tell them apart by simply looking at them, Harry stared at the ground, looking for any sign of fallen walnuts.

After searching for several moments, he saw the first one. It was old and rotting; its shell black and mostly cracked. He bent over and picked it up, rolling it around between his fingers. He looked around the immediate area and saw several more, in the same rotten condition. They all seemed to surround one large tree. It had several branches that, like the other trees, had been stripped of its leaves. The stripped branches looked like long, skinny arms trying to touch the sky. He was sure that when the tree had its leaves, it might be quite beautiful. But right now, as Harry stood beneath it, he thought it was, maybe, the scariest-looking tree he had ever seen.

A few stubborn walnuts still clung to the branches, and something about the way they looked still suspended in the air made the tree look even creepier. *Well, here's the walnut tree,* Harry thought. *Now what?*

He looked back to the old paper again and read the next line:

Beneath it all, a large stone face
with eyes that cannot see.

"Beneath it all," Harry said with a waver in his voice. He wasn't exactly sure what that meant, but he figured the walnut tree was still involved. Otherwise, why would the tree even be mentioned in the poem?

He started to look around the base of the tree, wondering if there might be some sort of secret trap door that led to an underground bunker or something. It was a very exciting idea, and within a few seconds, Harry nearly forgot that he was actually on Mayor Kligore's property when he should have been in school. He was on an adventure, a magic quest that no one else could know about.

Still, he realized the trouble and danger he could get in. As he hunted around the trunk of the walnut tree, he wished Rabbit were there with him. Rabbit tended to come and go when he pleased, sometimes appearing at random and unexpected times—especially when Harry needed advice or assistance.

Harry wondered where Rabbit was right now and what he was doing.

As Harry came to the back of the tree, he saw something quite peculiar. Right along the ground, where the large roots of the tree sank into the ground, there appeared to be a hollow between the base of the tree and the ground. The hole was roughly three feet wide and two feet tall. Although it was very dark within the hollow, Harry sensed that it

64

went into the tree and then sank down into the ground with the roots.

With a bravery and recklessness that only thirteen-year-old boys possess, Harry peered into the hollow. As he had assumed, it was pitch black. He could feel cobwebs and dirt pressing against his face. A thick, earthy smell filled the hole, and it made him feel like he had to sneeze. He drew his head back out and peered down into the darkness, thinking.

With his wand still in hand, Harry kept his eyes trained on the darkness. He thought hard, trying to summon a series of words—a magical code of sorts that might help him. Often, the words came to him like an unexpected breeze. But now he had to search for them, struggling to pull them from the very air around him.

65

Slowly, they came to him. As they did, he peered to the MagiKwest countdown clock which was now at 17:57. Sure, it was plenty of time, but Harry had no idea how he was supposed to get *"beneath it all."*

With the words now in his head, Harry poked his head back into the dark hole within the walnut tree. He extended his wand into the darkness and spoke the words.

"The dark is thick within this tree;
provide me light so that I can see!"

Harry felt something stirring from within his wand. Within seconds, a small orange spark erupted from its tip. With it, a small colony of fireflies was birthed into the darkness. They hovered in the darkness, shedding a pleasant, orange light. There were about twenty of them in all, and while their combined light was not nearly as powerful as a flashlight beam, they provided more than enough light for Harry to see.

He looked down into the hole and saw a series of roots from the walnut tree that reached down into the earth. They wound over one another, creating a weird sort of ladder. The trick, though, was getting to the ladder without falling down through the hole.

Am I really even thinking about going down there? Harry asked himself.

He was shocked and delighted to find that he was. He was *so* enthralled with the idea of a magical scavenger hunt that he was pretty sure there wasn't much of anything he *wouldn't* do.

He'd need both hands to get down there, so he placed his wand in his book bag and his phone in his pocket. He scooted back into the hole and felt the earth start to drop out from under him when he was about halfway through. He had to scrunch his legs up to fit fully inside and then reached out for the first of the roots. The fireflies still lit up the place with their pretty, orange glow, and something about it made this whole insane idea seem a bit safer.

He managed to twist his body around and then, holding to the first root, let his legs fall over into the hole. He panicked for just a moment but then relaxed when his feet found purchase on the next gnarled root beneath him. He started to climb down, the roots sagging a bit under his weight. As he climbed further down into the earth, the fireflies followed. They danced in the air, apparently just as excited to be on this adventure as Harry was.

He climbed down for what seemed like several minutes when he started to wonder just how far down this ladder went. He looked up and realized that, even with the glow of the fireflies to help, he could no longer see the light from outside of the tree. When he started to wonder just how deep beneath the ground he was, he began to feel scared.

But the fireflies continued to dance, urging him on. Harry took a moment to collect his nerves and then continued to climb down into the waiting darkness below.

IN THE UNDERGROUND

Just when Harry started to feel absolutely certain that the hole would go on forever, his foot landed on something solid. He looked down and, by the fireflies' light, saw that he had come to an old wooden floor. Standing on it, he saw that it led only one way, reaching back into a narrow tunnel that had been carved directly out of the dirt and rock of the earth. The fireflies wandered ahead of him a bit, illuminating the tunnel.

Harry took a moment to feel the quiet and stillness of the place. It seemed to be a bit hotter now. While everything *seemed* safe, Harry still took his wand out. Just in case.

As he stepped into the tunnel, he also took out his cell phone to check his time. He blinked in surprise when he saw that the MagiKwest clock was now down to 08:12.

Harry quickened his pace, heading farther into the tunnel. His feet made deep, echoing sounds against the wooden floor as he followed along behind the fireflies. As he raced forward, he once again looked at the paper he'd gotten from the graveyard. He read it in the flickering light from his new bug friends, trying to make sense of it.

Beneath it all, a large stone face
with eyes that cannot see.

Just as he looked up from the paper,

reciting the words over and over in his head, something huge came out of the darkness at him.

Harry let out a scream and came to a halt. He slid on the wooden floor and landed hard on his backside. He scrambled away, nearly screaming again, but then realized what he was seeing. And while it made no real sort of sense, it was certainly not anything to be scared of.

71

Embarrassed, Harry got back to his feet and took a few steps forward. Directly ahead of him, the fireflies were glowing around what looked like the head of a very large statue. The head was made of granite or some other sort of rock and looked as if it had been beheaded from a much larger statue.

It was not the head of a man from what Harry could see. But it also didn't look like a monster. No . . . this was something in between. Its eyes were drawn out in mean-looking slits, and its nose was huge. But its mouth was the most menacing thing; it was opened in a snarl, revealing a set of razor-sharp teeth and a tongue that hung out like a snake.

Well, there's the stone face, Harry thought, stepping forward and placing his hand on the statue's big, beast-like snout.

He looked up at the eyes—which, presumably, could not see—and saw nothing of particular interest about them. Not at first, anyway . . .

After staring for a while, Harry *did* see something slightly unnatural about the statue's slanted eyes. He had to stand directly in front of it, but he could see what looked like a series of small, silver squares on its eyes. There were three in each eye: one in the right corner, one in the pupil, and one in the left corner. Within each of the silver squares, a number had been engraved.

Harry quickly brought out the paper from the graveyard again and looked at the number that had made no sense to him when he had unlocked the compartment on the back of Henry David Thoreau's headstone.

Harry got on his tiptoes but was unable to reach the statue's eyes. It was that tall. Thinking quickly, Harry locked his hands around the thing's huge nose and pulled himself up. His feet scrambled against the thing's face as he

73

climbed. When his foot slipped over the thing's bottom lip, Harry shivered. Even if it was only a statue, the idea of his foot being in the stone creature's mouth was eerie.

After some struggling, Harry finally managed to hoist himself up onto the statue's nose. He leaned forward against the face and balanced himself on its nose. He set the paper on one knee and his phone on the other. The MagiKwest countdown clock was now at 3:09.

With a new sense of urgency, Harry set to work. He placed his hand on the first silver square and found that he could roll it up or down. It made a slight clicking noise when he moved it, and as he locked in the first number, Harry realized that this was a combination lock that was exactly like the one on his dad's work briefcase.

He locked in the first set of numbers on the creature's right eye: 5, 6, 1. Then, with his heart fluttering and the countdown clock now reaching 2:30, he locked in the numbers on the second eye: *9, 9, 4.*

The moment he rolled the last silver square to 4, the big granite head started to rumble. It was so sudden and unexpected that Harry fell off of the thing's nose and hit the wooden floor hard. He let out an oof as he scooted back to see what was about to happen. Over his head, the fireflies had gone still.

A deep, groaning sound filled the tunnel, so loud that Harry felt like it was actually in his head. As the sound got even louder, the statue began to open its mouth. The sound of its granite jaws grinding together was terrible, but the sight of the statue opening its mouth was still very cool.

"Whoa," Harry said as the mouth stopped stretching open.

There was one final booming noise as the statue's jaws locked into place. Harry slowly got to his feet and realized that the opened mouth was taller than he was.

It was obvious what he needed to do, but Harry wasn't sure if he could do it. Sure, he had come this far and had some very intense fun but . . . something about the way the big granite face looked seemed very off-putting to Harry—especially now that it had its mouth wide open.

He looked at his phone, which had clattered on the floor, and saw that the countdown clock had stopped with just 0:45 on it. Beneath the countdown clock was a brief message that made Harry's decision so much easier.

> You're almost there! Soon you'll have the secrets to the greatest magic in the world. Keep at it! Run, Harry, run!

Knowing that there was no turning back now, Harry readjusted his book bag, took his wand out again, and headed for the open mouth of the statue. The fireflies went with him, staying close and giving off their orange glow. They made him feel a little more confident as he stepped over the statue's bottom jaw.

"Harry, wait!"

The voice came out of nowhere. It was familiar and instantly made Harry feel safe. But at the same time, it also made him feel very guilty. He turned slowly, looking behind him.

Rabbit was there, looking at him with deep concern. It was the same sort of concern Harry sometimes saw in his mother when she was worried about him. Harry had not heard Rabbit come up behind him. While Rabbit was usually very quiet and moved around almost like a ghost, Harry could usually sense where he was. But this time, Rabbit had come to him by total surprise.

"Rabbit," he said. "What are you doing here?"

"I should ask you the same thing," Rabbit said. "Why are you not in school?"

Harry didn't answer. There was something in Rabbit's eyes that suggested Rabbit already knew the answer. "I have something else to do," Harry said.

"I can see that," Rabbit said. "But do you think it's the best idea?"

"I don't know," Harry said. "But . . . well . . . this is none of your business, Rabbit. This is something I want to do . . . and I need to do it on my own."

"Are you sure about that, Harry?"

"Yes," Harry said.

He very badly wanted to yell at Rabbit and tell Rabbit to leave him alone. But the guilt he felt now was one hundred times worse than what he had felt when he'd lied to the Good Mischief Team. He knew it was not like him, but in that moment, he simply did not care. It was almost like someone was controlling him, pushing buttons on a video game controller that caused him to act differently.

"Come home, Harry," Rabbit pleaded. "Before it's too late."

Harry looked down into that cavernous mouth in front of him. He then looked at the fireflies dancing around his head. It was all so awesome . . . so magical. He wasn't about to turn away from it all now.

"No," Harry said, almost like a hiss. "Go away, Rabbit."

Rabbit only nodded. He didn't seem sad or upset, though his ears drooped slightly. "Very well," he said. "It's clear you've made your choice."

Rabbit turned and hopped away back into the darkness. Harry nearly called out for him, to ask him to please come along the rest of the way with him. But he bit his lip when he realized that meant he'd have to tell Rabbit all about MagiKwest—and that was a big no-no.

Nearly in tears, Harry looked away from the murky shape of Rabbit hopping into the shadows and turned back to the statue and its wide, gaping mouth.

Inside the thing's mouth, it was very dark . . . darker than the hollow in the walnut tree, even. He took another step into the thing's mouth and realized that not even the fireflies were able to penetrate this darkness.

"It's very dark in here," he said, partly to himself and partly to the fireflies. "I wonder if it—"

But then his feet ran out of floor and there was nothing left to support him. He felt the world drop out from under his feet, and the intense feeling of falling snatched the last few words right out of his mouth.

He fell and fell and fell some more and couldn't even draw in a breath to scream.

Much like the ladder of roots, Harry wondered if this hole would ever end. And when it did, what would he hit? He imagined the pain and winced against it even as he continued to fall.

With horrifying clarity, he could picture himself walking into the mouth of the statue. And now that he was falling, he wondered if he was *really* falling at all . . . or had he been *swallowed?*

With that terrible thought in his mind, Harry started to feel something very much like sleepiness wash over him and after that, there was just the dark.

81

82

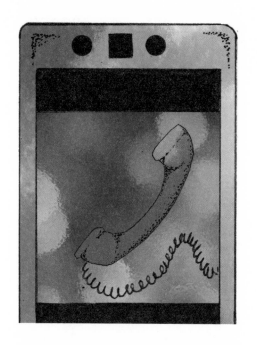

MARY MOON AND THE GOOD MISCHIEF TEAM

When Mary Moon got home from work and found that Harry was not there, she did not worry at first. It was nothing new for Harry to go visit with his friends after school. So long as his homework got done, Mary and John Moon did not mind him having a bit of fun once the school day was over.

Honey Moon was sitting on the couch when Mary got home. Honey was reading a book and having her usual afternoon snack of apples and peanut butter.

"How was school, dear?" Mary asked as she entered the house. She was carrying Harvest, the youngest of the three Moon siblings, on her hip, having picked him up from daycare after work.

"Good. How was work?"

"Good." She took a moment to look around for Harry and then asked, "Where's your brother?"

Honey shrugged. "I don't know. I haven't seen him all afternoon. I figured he was at Declan's."

"Probably," Mary said. She had good kids and trusted them most of the time. Mary just wished he would have sent her a text or left a note.

After putting Harvest at the table for his afternoon snack, Mary took out her cell phone and sent Harry a text.

Where are you?

She set the phone down on the kitchen table and then started searching through the cupboards for a dinner idea. After that, the evening went as it usually did in the Moon household. Honey came to the table and did her homework. When she was done, she helped Mary prepare dinner. Harvest, meanwhile, played with building blocks in the living room. About forty minutes after Mary got home, John came in through the front door. He was carrying his briefcase, which meant he'd probably have some work to do tonight.

Mary looked at the clock and realized that it was getting late. It was closing in on 5:30, and she had not yet heard from Harry. And he still had to do his homework before dinner!

85

Irritated now, and really not wanting to have to gripe at Harry, she went back to her phone. She dialed Harry's number, but when she put the phone to her ear, she heard just a few clicks. He was either out of range or his battery was dead. Now growing angry, she sighed and pulled up Declan Dickinson's home phone number. It was answered on the second ring by Mrs. Dickinson.

"Hi, this is Mary Moon," she said, trying to sound as casual as possible. "I was wondering if Harry was over there by any chance."

"No, he's not," Mrs. Dickinson said. "Hao is here, though. He and Declan have been playing all afternoon. No sign of Harry, though."

"Oh," Mary said. For the first time, a sharp jab of worry spiraled through her. "Well, thanks."

"Is everything okay?" Mrs. Dickinson asked.

"Oh, sure. I think Harry has just lost track of time out on one of his little adventures."

"Oh, I know how that goes," Mrs. Dickinson said with a laugh.

"Thanks again," Mary said, ending the call.

She scrolled through her numbers again, this time pulling up Bailey Wheeler's home number. As it started to ring in her ear, John Moon poked his head into the kitchen with a worried scowl on his face.

"Everything okay?" he asked.

87

Mary did not get a chance to answer. The phone at the Wheeler's house was answered. She recognized Bailey's voice at once. "Hello?" he said.

"Hey, Bailey, this is Mary Moon . . . Harry's mom."

"Oh, hi, Mrs. Moon. What's up?"

"I'm trying to get in touch with Harry. He hasn't come home yet, and I figured he was with you or one of your friends."

"He's not here," Bailey said, sounding confused. "Um, actually, Mrs. Moon . . . Harry wasn't at school today."

Worry turned into panic, filling Mary's stomach like a big rock. "What?" she said.

"Yeah, we thought it was weird too," Bailey replied. "He was fine yesterday. But when we saw him while walking to school this morning, he said he wasn't feeling good. He turned around and went back home."

"*What?* Well, he's not here right now." She thought for a moment, trying to push the worry away and then added, "Did he speak to any of you on the phone last night?"

"No, ma'am."

"Okay," Mary said, her voice shaking slightly, like cornstalks in the breeze.

"Is he okay?" Bailey asked. He sounded worried.

"I'll let you know when I find him," Mary said. "Thanks, Bailey."

When she hung up the phone, John and Honey were looking at her with concerned expressions. Even Harvest tottered into the kitchen, sensing something was wrong.

"Mary?" John asked. "What is it?"

Doing her best to keep from crying, Mary

sat down heavily in a chair at the kitchen table. "I think we need to call the police," she said. "Harry is missing."

When Harry had still not arrived home by 8:15, the police search for him involved every police car in Sleepy Hollow. There were only three, but it was very rare that they were all out on patrol at the same time. The chief of police had stopped by the Moon house twice. Mary could tell that he was almost as worried as she was. A missing child wasn't something that ever happened in Sleepy Hollow. Suddenly, their sleepy, little town seemed like a dark and sinister place.

When the chief had stopped by at 8:50 with no news or updates, Mary allowed herself to cry. She did it in the bathroom, though, so Harvest and Honey would not see her. She needed to appear strong and confident for them—allowing them the hope that Harry was still okay. John came in with her and hugged her tightly, and she could tell that he was also doing everything he could to not start crying as well.

Their bathroom crying session was interrupted by the ringing of the doorbell. Praying that it was Harry or the police chief with some good news, Mary dashed to the front door. When she opened it, she did not see Harry, but there *were* three familiar faces on her doorstep.

Declan, Bailey, and Hao stood there under the glow of the Moon porch light. They all looked very sad but not nearly as wrecked as Mary felt.

91

"Hi, Mrs. Moon," Hao said.

"Hi, boys," Mary said. "Do your parents know you're here?"

"Yes, ma'am," Declan said. "But we have to be back soon. We wanted to come over to let you know that we're pretty sure Harry is okay."

"He is?" Mary said. "How do you know?"

"Well, we don't know for sure," Bailey said.

"Yeah, but it's *Harry*," Hao said. "Nothing could ever happen to Harry. He's too good, you know? He's strong and brave."

"Oh, I know," Mary said, fighting not to cry in front of these boys.

"We also wanted you to know that we want to help if we can," Hao said.

"I don't think there's anything you *can* do," Mary said. "But the gesture is very sweet."

"We can keep our eyes and ears open at school," Declan said. "Maybe someone else at school knows where he is."

"Yeah," Bailey said. "I'd start by asking the Kligore brothers."

"Now, boys," Mary said. "This is no time to be making accusations. Right now, we just have to hope and pray. The police are doing their jobs well. I feel confident that we'll have Harry

back safe and sound very soon."

The boys nodded in unison, but they did not seem so sure.

"Now, get back home," Mary said. "It was very sweet of you to visit, but there's nothing you can do now."

Again, they nodded. "Goodnight, Mrs. Moon," they all said together as they stepped back down to the yard and retrieved their bikes.

93

Mary watched them pedal away in the moonlight and frowned deeply. She'd always been honest with Harry and his friends . . . until now. She had just told then that she felt like Harry would be back home, safe and sound, very soon.

But as each minute passed and the night grew darker around them, she wasn't sure that was true.

Riding their bikes under the cover of

night made the other members of the Good Mischief Team feel like spies or great detectives. Still, with the core member of their group missing, it was hard to find much joy in it.

As they approached Declan's house, they slowed their bikes and spoke in hushed tones. "So what do you think happened to him?" Hao asked.

"I don't know," Bailey said. "But this isn't like Harry. He'd never skip school, and he'd *never* make his parents worry like that."

"He's got to be in trouble then, right?" Declan suggested.

"Probably," Bailey said.

All three of them went quiet. Declan looked up to the moon—three-quarters full tonight—because it always reminded him of Harry.

"There has to be something we can do," Declan said.

"We can grill Titus Kligore at school tomorrow," Hao said. "If Harry is missing, that creep probably knows about it."

All three boys felt the same way, but they also knew that to actually come out and suggest this to anyone other than Mary Moon could get them in trouble.

"Well, I need to get home," Declan said, turning his bike toward his house. They could all see his mom standing at the door, highlighted by the lights that were on in the house.

"See you tomorrow," Hao said.

"Say a prayer for Harry before bed," Bailey said.

"Will do," Declan said. "Good night, guys."

Bailey and Hao started off, heading for Bailey's house. They said nothing and rode in silence. Anyone that happened to pass them would likely notice their hunched shoulders

95

and lack of energy. Even hidden in the dark of night, it was clear that the two boys were sad, riding through the night as if they had lost a very large part of themselves.

The doorbell at the Moon home rang again twenty minutes after the Good Mischief Team had left. John Moon was busy trying to keep Honey from crying over her missing brother, so that left Mary to answer the door. Harvest, usually asleep by this time, was in her arms. He was clearly tired, but even he seemed to understand that something bad was happening.

When Mary answered the door, she saw Samson Dupree standing at her doorstep. He gave her a smile that was somehow bright yet full of sadness. She nearly started crying at the sight of him. Samson had been the one that had told her, soon after Harry was born, that her son was destined for great things.

"Hello, Mary," he said. "I wonder if I might speak with you in private?"

"Sure," she said, stifling back a sob. With Harvest in her arms, she stepped out onto the porch. The night was a little chilly, but she hardly noticed.

"I heard about Harry," he said. "I wish to offer my deepest sympathies . . . but also some hope."

"I could use some of that," she said.

"Harry, as you know, is quite special. He's very much a thirteen-year-old boy, and he goes through the same growing pains as all of his friends. But, being as special as he is, I think you must also know that he will undergo some obstacles in his young life that his friends may never have to."

"Samson . . . do you know something about Harry? Do you know where he is?"

"I'm afraid not," he said. "But I have a sort of connection to him, as you know. If anything had happened to him, I would know."

"What sort of connection?" Mary asked. She hefted Harvest over to her other hip as he reached out with a chubby hand and swatted at Samson's robes.

"I'm not quite sure of that myself," he said. "I'm still learning. But I think you need to know that someone as special as Harry will usually find himself tempted and lured by dark things."

"What?"

"I don't say that to frighten you, Mary Moon. But as most young men start dealing with crushes on girls, violent movies, and disrespecting their parents, Harry has to deal with other things. And like most young teens, he likely feels he has to face some of those things alone."

"But he keeps doing it," she said. "Whatever talent he has been gifted with, why does he have to be the one to always go head-on into danger?"

"Because he has great faith. And the boy is

the bravest person I have ever known."

"He *is* that," Mary said with a smile.

"Don't fret, Mary. I *sense* there are more great things ahead for Harry. And that being said, I do believe he will return home to you."

"But when?"

"That, I do not know."

She nodded. Although Samson had offered no proof that Harry was alright, his mere presence and words of assurance were enough for Mary at that moment. "Thank you, Samson."

"Of course. Is there anything else I can do for you?"

She shrugged. "Just pray that he returns home safely."

"Oh, I pray for Harry constantly. A boy of his stature . . . he often needs it."

"That's for sure," Mary said. "Goodnight,

Samson."

"And you, as well, Mary."

Mary closed the door and looked into the empty living room. She could barely hear John upstairs, talking in soft tones to Honey. She had been crying earlier but now seemed to have it down to a series of wet sniffles.

In her arms, Harvest also looked around, as if confused. "Where Harry?" he asked in his cute little sing-song voice. "Where Harry? He go abracadabra!"

Mary smiled, but it only stayed on her face for a few moments before it morphed into a frown, and she was crying again. As she went to the couch and wept, little Harvest buried his face into her shoulder and did the only thing he could think to do: he hugged his mother as tightly as he could, sensing that she was deeply troubled.

DEMON DOGS

Harry opened his eyes and realized that his throat was sore. He remembered screaming a lot. He also remembered falling for what seemed like forever . . . that was why he had been screaming. It all came rushing back to him then—stepping into the mouth of that creepy statue, taking a few steps, and then falling.

Harry tried sitting up but realized that something was holding him. Overhead, the light of the fireflies still flickered down on him. By their light, Harry could see that he was being held by what looked like roots. They were not holding him down, but supporting him. A canopy of them was under his back, and a few were wrapped securely over his shoulder. He could barely remember the shapes of these arm-like roots coming out of the darkness as he fell. He'd blacked out shortly after seeing them, afraid that they were the tentacles of some beast from deep within the earth.

Harry was able to easily remove the roots from his shoulders. He sat up and found his wand resting in the roots as well. He picked it up in the way a toddler might pick up their favorite blanket while in the dark.

He peered up at the fireflies, waiting for them to move. When they did not, he sighed and said, "I think I need to go lower," he said. "What's down there?"

The fireflies seemed hesitant. It was clear that they had no interest in going any deeper underground. But at Harry's urging, they did so. Something about their light seemed sad and afraid as they passed by Harry's odd nest of roots and deeper into the darkness. As they passed by, the net of roots started to come undone, following them down.

Sensing the peculiar roots that had likely saved his life were starting to unravel, Harry quickly held on to the thickest root near him. He grabbed it with both hands, after putting his wand between his teeth. The root finally dropped away from the rest of the root net, swinging Harry slowly to the left. Thanks to the fireflies, he saw a rock wall waiting for him. He kicked out his legs and bounced harmlessly from it. He then looked down and was relieved to see rocky ground waiting beneath him.

With his hands still gripping the root, Harry half-walked and half-bounced his way down the rock wall. As he did, he got the sense that he was somewhere beyond deep now. He was further down inside the earth than he had ever even imagined. It was getting very hot, and it felt stuffy.

Still, when his feet were on the rocky ground, he managed to relax a little bit. Somewhere in the back of his mind, he wondered how he would get back up. But that was a problem for another time.

He looked at his phone and saw that the MagiKwest app wasn't much help. The countdown clock was now just a series of dashes, and he had no messages waiting for him. There was, however, a flashing arrow. It was pointing straight ahead.

Harry shrugged and started walking forward. The fireflies were still his only source of light, but his eyes had become accustomed to their little bit of shine, and it was more than enough. He found himself walking into a cavern of sorts, a large opening in a massive granite wall. Here and there, a few flickering shards of rock poked through the wall of the cavern. Harry wondered if they were diamonds. Surely there was gold, diamonds, and other undiscovered riches down here in the deeper parts of the earth.

After a few minutes, Harry came to a place in the cavern where another tunnel opened up. He had to choose either left or right. He looked down at his phone and saw that the MagiKwest app was telling him to go left. He did so, the fireflies floating dutifully behind him.

He had walked for no more than ten seconds before this tunnel widened into a huge opening. He looked up and saw rocks and odd, stony formations overhead. In front of him, there were six tunnels. A few of them looked too small to pass through, but the others were huge. As he started walking toward them, hoping the MagiKwest app would again tell him where to go, Harry thought he heard something to his right.

He paused, not sure what the sound had been. It came again, and he realized it was coming from one of the smaller tunnels. Curious, he walked over to the tunnel's entrance, hoping to hear it better. He got down on his knees, leaned his head into the tunnel, and listened.

Now, he could tell what the sound was. And it made his eyes go wide with fear.

Growling. It was growling . . . and it was getting closer.

Harry scrambled to his feet and looked at the MagiKwest app again. Now, a flashing arrow was telling him to take the large tunnel farthest to the right. Harry thought about the message he had seen on the app so often, and it seemed to blare through his head.

Run, Harry, run!

He started running to the right as the arrow instructed, but the sound of the growling grew louder than ever.

As he reached the tunnel, he looked back over his shoulder and saw a dark shape emerge from the smaller tunnel he'd been kneeling in front of only seconds ago. He wasn't sure what the shape was, but he did know that, whatever it was, it was making the growling noise. And it was chasing after him.

Harry sped into the tunnel to the right and ran as fast as he could. The fireflies kept up, their speedy light casting Harry's murky shadow along the wall as he ran. He continued to hear the growling behind him, and even though he knew it was a bad idea, he couldn't help but look back over his shoulder. This time, he turned on his cell phone, using its glow for additional light.

The light revealed that the shape chasing after him was actually two shapes. It was hard to be certain in the murky light, but Harry was pretty sure there were two huge dogs coming after him. As if to prove this, one of them gave out a thunderous bark as Harry flashed his cell phone light at them.

The purest fear Harry had ever felt flooded his heart. It sent electric charges of energy into his legs, allowing him to run a bit faster. But, no matter how fast he ran, the dogs seemed to be faster. He could tell just from the sounds of their growls and barks that they were closing in fast.

On his phone, another arrow flashed. This one told him that there was a turn coming up, and he should go right. He did so, the orange blur of fireflies trailing over his head. He was going so fast that he nearly collided with the wall when he turned.

When he corrected himself and started running straight again, there was a horrifying moment when Harry got a clear view of the dogs. While he knew they were dogs, they were so enormous that they looked more like little bears—little bears with blood-red eyes and fangs as sharp as knives. As they snarled at him, thick ropes of spit flew everywhere.

Harry could think of nothing to do. Nothing in the MagiKwest app had suggested that there would be monstrous hellhounds to contend with. He felt like he had been tricked—that the game had led him this far just to be chased down by these hellhounds.

He was going to have to use his magic. In the same way, he had used his magic to conjure up the fireflies, he was going to have to also use it to put a stop to these hellhounds.

His lungs seemed to be burning as he gripped his wand tightly, trying to think of the right words to use. He waited for them to come, feeling them sort themselves out within his panicked mind. As they did, Harry realized that he could now also hear the footsteps of the charging hounds, their claws clicking against the stone floor. Moments later, he was pretty sure he could feel their hot, stinking breath on the back of his neck.

110

Feeling the magic start to bubble up within his wand, Harry acted as quickly as he could, knowing that one wrong move could result in the hellhounds having him for dinner. He raised his wand while he was still running, opened his mouth, and recited the words that sprang to his tongue without so much as a thought.

> *"These frightening dogs,*
> *all hatred and rage,*
> *would seem much nicer*
> *from behind a cage."*

When he spoke the word cage, Harry

stopped running and fell directly to the ground. When he turned to look behind him, the hellhounds were nearly on him—the one in the lead was actually springing back on its haunches to leap at Harry.

Harry flicked his wand in their direction. A bright bolt of energy came spiraling out of his wand. It struck both dogs, and one of them let out a pitiful, little yipping noise.

When Harry realized that the dogs were still coming forward, wrapped up in some sort of magical cloud that was still taking shape, he rolled out of the way. When he did, he slammed directly into the rock wall. When he hit it, something else made a loud, clanging noise behind him. It was so loud he felt it in his bones.

When he got to his feet, he looked at the hellhounds and couldn't help but smile. The spell had conjured up a large, steel cage. Both dogs were pouting behind the bars, utterly confused. They still looked monstrous but knew they had been bested. Their fangs were now hidden by their pouting lips, and their red eyes looked sad.

Harry took a moment to catch his breath. After a while, the fear and adrenaline that had been coursing through him finally tapered off. He slowly backed away from the cage, the hellhounds looking at him with pleading eyes, now not scary at all.

Harry then looked back to his phone. The MagiKwest app was telling him he needed to keep going straight. This time, a simple message appeared over the flashing arrow. It read, quite simply: ALMOST THERE.

Harry headed forward, a little slower than he had before. Now he got the sense that all of this had been a big mistake—a very big mistake.

He glanced down at his phone and saw the time. He couldn't believe his eyes. When he had entered the hollow of the tree at Folly Farm, it hadn't even been noon. And now, somehow, it was nearing midnight.

Mom and Dad are going to be so worried, he thought.

Feeling guilt for what he had done for the first time since getting that first text from MagiKwest, Harry kept walking forward, following the flashing arrow on his phone.

The fireflies followed somberly behind as if they, too, could feel the guilt and defeat that Harry Moon took with him deeper down into the earth.

113

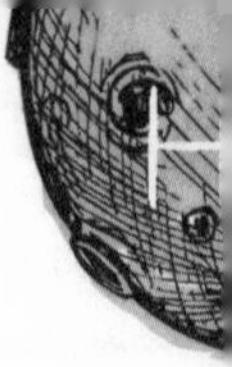

EVERYTHING HE
EVER WANTED

Harry was starting to get really hungry. He was thirsty, too. Realizing this, he suddenly felt very foolish. He sat down on the rock floor and slid his book bag from his shoulders. He reached inside and withdrew his lunchbox. He always packed his lunch the night before school. Sometimes it made his sandwiches a little cold and limp, but it was much better than being rushed in the morning.

Harry ate the ham and cheese sandwich and the apple that he had packed over twenty-four hours ago. He washed it down with a juice box. The juice was pretty warm by now, but it still made him forget about being thirsty.

116

With his quick lunch (or dinner or whatever people tended to eat at 11:48 p.m.) done, Harry slung his book bag over his shoulder and continued on into the darkness. He'd made it no more than five steps before the tunnel he was in made a downward shift. It was so steep that Harry had to almost climb down it rather than walk.

It took a few moments, but when he was finally at the bottom, he got a very weird feeling. He felt that he was almost there. He had no idea how he knew it, but he thought this journey was almost over. He checked the MagiKWest app to see if it had anything to say,

but it still only showed the flashing arrow and the message:

ALMOST THERE.

The fireflies still seemed to hesitate. As far as Harry was concerned, the fact that they seemed afraid was perhaps the worst hint of all that he had stumbled into something bad. He scolded himself as he walked further into the caverns. *How could I have been so stupid? How could I have been so irresponsible?*

131

"Oh, don't do that to yourself, Harry."

The voice came out of nowhere, freezing Harry in place. And although he could not see who had spoken, he knew the voice very well. It was a voice that usually made his heart stutter in his chest and his stomach feel like it was in knots.

It was Sarah Sinclair. But what was she doing down here?

"Sarah?" he asked. "Is that you?"

Sure enough, Sarah stepped out of the darkness just a few feet ahead of him. He could barely see her by the light of the fireflies, but what he saw was beautiful. Her blonde hair was barely spilling over her

shoulders, and something about the orangish firefly glow made her look even prettier than usual.

"Hi, Harry," she said, stepping even closer to him.

"Sarah, what are you doing down here?"

She smiled and then looked at the fireflies. She smirked as if she didn't trust them.

119

"It's all part of the game, Harry," she said. "MagiKwest has promised you the secret to being a great magician. And what would be the point of being a magician if you couldn't have everything you ever wanted?"

"I don't understand," Harry said.

"I know," she said. "But you will soon enough."

She stepped closer to him, close enough to touch now, and Harry sensed that there was something very wrong with Sarah. He couldn't quite put his finger on it, but Sarah seemed . . . off somehow.

"We both know you like me, Harry," she said. She smiled at him as she took a step closer to him. "And we both know why you and I just wouldn't work. You're too young. People wouldn't understand. But if you were a great magician . . . well, we could fix that. And I could be your girlfriend. Isn't that what you want, Harry?"

In fact, it was one of the things Harry had always wanted. She wasn't just pretty . . . Sarah was smart, funny, and genuinely kind. But here in the darkness of this place, none of that seemed right. Down here . . . he was pretty sure something was wrong with Sarah.

"Sarah," he said. "Have you seen my mom? Is she worried? Is she—"

Sarah reached out and took his hand. It was ice cold despite the heat of the tunnel.

"Just forget about all of that," Sarah said.

"You're so close to being a great magician, Harry. The power down here that is waiting for you is more than you could ever imagine. You and I could be together. You and your friends could be very powerful. You could rule Sleepy Hollow."

She was very close to him now. She was leaning down, and their faces were so close that their noses were almost touching.

And that's when Harry saw it. There was something in Sarah's eyes that wasn't right. Actually, there was something in Sarah's eyes that made him understand that this was not Sarah Sinclair. This wasn't his Sarah at all. Her excitement for life and the kind twinkle he had seen in her eyes so many times was not there. In its place was something dull and nearly dead. It looked . . . well, it looked fake.

"Who are you?" Harry asked, a bit heartbroken that he'd been fooled in such a way.

She shrugged, and Harry sensed that she (or it or whatever this thing was) knew

121

that Harry had figured it out. The fake Sarah shrugged again and gave him a smile. "Silly boy," she said. "I'm everything you ever wanted."

"No, I don't think so," Harry said, bringing his wand up. "In fact, I think this whole MagiKwest thing is just like you; it's all fake!"

He gave a wave of his wand and shouted: "ABRACADABRA!"

In an instant, the thing that was not Sarah Sinclair became a cloud of dust. It all fell to the floor quietly. Harry looked down at it with a frown. He bent down and ran his hands through it before looking up at the fireflies. A large part of him was saddened that he had been tricked and still another part of him wished it had been Sarah. He could have used a friendly face down here in the dark.

He looked at the ashes on his hands and wiped them on his pants. He then peered into the darkness ahead of him. He had never felt so alone in his life.

"What do you think?" he asked the fireflies. "Should we head back and try to get home?"

The fireflies, of course, did not answer him.

His phone buzzed in his pocket. He took it out and saw that he had a new message from MagiKwest. The arrow still flashed, pointing forward, but the message had changed.

Now it read: You have an appointment in 3 minutes.

An appointment? With who? Harry wondered.

He checked the time, and a little shudder passed through him when he saw that it was 11:57. In three minutes, it would be midnight.

The end was near . . . the game was nearly over. Harry felt it, just as surely as he felt the sorrow of having been fooled by a fake Sarah.

The fireflies led the way as Harry ventured forward, heading into the darkness for his midnight appointment.

124

SPEAKING SHADOWS
AND A FLUFFY TAIL

ary Moon knew she wasn't sick, but that's how she felt. It was 11:59, and she felt feverish. Her stomach was also upset, and she was beginning to feel tired. She supposed this was what grief felt like—what it felt like to have no idea where her very special son had disappeared to.

When the police had still not had any leads at 10:30, she nearly fell asleep on the couch. She guessed she was emotionally tired, because she didn't know how on earth she would have managed to fall asleep otherwise. Her boy was out there somewhere, in the night, missing and probably in some sort of trouble. It just wasn't like Harry to run off or to do anything at all without running it by her and John first.

John had led her into the bedroom and helped her into bed. He was manning the phones, making calls, and waiting hopefully for the police to call with good news. He insisted that she get some rest because the stress was already taking its toll on her.

When the clock showed 12:00 midnight and she was still not asleep, she nearly got out of bed. But the thought of going out there and doing nothing more than crying while staring at the front door, hoping Harry would come through it at any minute, was too sad for her. So she stayed there in bed, thinking about the day in the park not long after Harry was born. A man named Samson—a man Harry had lately come to call a friend and mentor—had approached her and told her that her son was going to be special. Samson had said Harry would endure trials and hardships that other kids his age would never have to face.

Had Samson been talking about this? Had he been talking about Harry going missing for unknown reasons? She had never really considered it before, but she did now because it was much easier to assume that he was off doing something special rather than getting into trouble or danger. In the back of her mind, she made a note to pay a visit to Samson to see if she could get some answers. Up until now, she had been fine with living with the mystery of it all. But now her boy was missing, and her world felt like it had been turned upside down.

"Harry," she said quietly into the room, his name really nothing more than a sob. "Please come home, Harry."

As soon as she said this, something close

by the bed moved. She sat up, a cry rising up in her throat, as she saw a shape at the foot of the bed. It was short and frightening at first, a blob of darkness in the already dark room. But then she saw the weird V-shape at the top of it and watched as one side of the "V" drooped sadly.

"Harry will be okay, Mary," this shape said.

She wanted to be afraid but knew that she was safe. That voice . . . she thought she'd heard it somewhere before or maybe dreamed it. It was soft and reassuring. It made her feel calm. It made her feel at ease.

"Who are you?" she asked.

There was jostling at the end of the bed as the shape jumped up onto the mattress. Mary reached for the lamp on her bedside table, but the voice at the end of the bed stopped her.

"Please don't," the shape said. "I think it's best you not see me clearly."

129

She thought this was a good idea. Still, as her eyes focused on the shape, more of it came into view. She started to recognize the shape, right down to the broken "V" on top of its head. And unless her eyes were deceiving her, she was pretty sure there was a perfectly round, fluffy tail along the bottom. It made no sense at all, but she was beginning to understand that there was a very large rabbit sitting on the end of her bed.

It has to be the stress, she thought. It has

to be . . .

But then again, she'd heard Harry speaking to someone every now and then . . . an imaginary friend, perhaps. But she also knew what Harry called that so-called imaginary friend. He called it Rabbit. And if Mary was honest with herself, hadn't she sometimes caught the shape of something furry and short natured just out of the corner of her eye when Harry was in her presence every now and then?

"Who are you?" Mary asked.

"My name is not important," the maybe-rabbit said. "Harry just calls me Rabbit. He and I have a bond—a connection, you might say."

"What sort of connection?"

"I go to him when he needs me. I lend a rather large ear when he needs someone to confide in and encouraging words when they are needed."

"Are you part of my imagination?" she asked.

"Sure," Rabbit said. "Let's go with that."

"But you said Harry will be okay?"

"Yes."

"How do you know?"

"I can't put it into words. It's something I feel. I think he is in a very bad place, in a bad situation. But Harry is strong. I wish I could be with him to help him. But I can't . . . not this time. This is something Harry must face alone. Right now, I believe you need me more."

131

"But you aren't even real," Mary scoffed. "You're a delusion brought on by stress."

"Maybe," he said. "But often, people in stress don't realize what sort of help they need until they have come to a breaking point."

In the back of her head, Mary recalled

something she'd heard along those lines in church one time. It made her feel safer, like maybe this had all been designed—maybe not a talking rabbit perched at the end of her bed but her having to suffer through Harry's disappearance.

"Will he come back home?" she asked. Finally, she could feel sleep trying to steal over her.

"Oh, I have no doubt. Harry is resilient. He's a good boy, Mary."

132

"He's the best," she said. "And he's special. That man said so. Samson."

Although she could not clearly see Rabbit's face, she was pretty sure he was smiling.

"Sleep, Mary," Rabbit said. "I'll be here, lurking about. I'll watch over you until your boy comes home."

Even if the rabbit was just a figment of her imagination, she believed him when he said this.

Mary might have smiled. She wasn't sure. She suddenly fell asleep, somehow sure she had already been asleep, because really, who on earth thought talking rabbits could just hop into anyone's bedroom and hold a conversation?

Mary Moon fell asleep, and the last thought she had before slumber took her over was how even though the rabbit had sounded hopeful, something about him had seemed sad—right down to the droopy ears.

134

THE BOSS

When the clock on Harry's phone read 11:59, he stepped into another large clearing. When his feet stepped onto the floor of this large cavern, a single overhead light came on. Harry looked up and saw that the light was *waaay* up at the top of the cavern, at least one hundred feet over

Harry's head.

   With the help of the overhead light, Harry could also see that the rock floor was no longer just made of rock. A large carpeted area was in front of him. At the other end of the carpeted space, there was a single desk. A woman sat behind it, typing something into a large computer. She seemed to not even notice that Harry was there.

   Confused beyond measure, Harry walked forward. As he did, the hot temperature of the underground cavern seemed to drop. It was much cooler now, almost like someone had turned on an unseen air conditioner. After he had taken a few steps forward, the woman at the desk looked up and noticed him. She was quite pretty, with raven black hair that seemed to slither elegantly on her head.

   "Well, hello there," the woman said. "Harry Moon, isn't it?"

   "Yes," he said uncertainly. He showed her his phone and said, "I have an appointment, I think."

"Of course you do," the woman said.

Yes, she was pretty, but there was something that Harry didn't like about her. Something in the way she smiled reminded Harry of the fake Sarah he had just encountered.

"Where am I?" Harry asked.

She grinned at him, revealing teeth as white as pearls and as menacing as a crocodile's. She clicked her fingers, and a sign lit up behind her. It was not a neon sign, but it seemed to glow from inside with light very similar to the fireflies that now hovered behind Harry.

The sign read: WE DRIVE BY NIGHT, INC.

"Come on now," the woman said. "Let's not keep him waiting."

"Let's not keep who waiting?" Harry asked.

The woman only laughed in response, like Harry had just told a joke. She got up from the desk and walked a few steps behind her desk. She clicked her fingers again, and a doorway was revealed. A simple placard sat on the side of the doorway with the words *THE BOSS* engraved into it.

The woman knocked and opened the door just a crack. "Boss man," she said through the small crack. "Your twelve o' clock is here."

A voice from inside the room drifted out like thunder. "Splendid. Thank you, Lady Dra Dra. Send him in!"

The woman, Lady Dra Dra, pushed the door open and gestured for Harry to go inside. Taking a deep breath, he stepped through the door. The room he stepped into was much smaller and looked like any plain, old office. He saw a desk on the other side of the room. A man was sitting there, his back to Harry.

As Harry started to walk forward, he felt his phone buzz in his pocket. He took it out and gave it a weird look. There was no message from MagiKwest. In fact, there were no alerts of any kind.

His phone had gone dead.

As soon as he realized this, the door behind him slammed closed.

Harry wheeled around and thought about trying to open it. But by then, he heard the man behind the desk moving.

"Not trying to leave already are you, Harry?" the man asked.

Harry turned and saw the man for the first time. He was slightly overweight and looked to be about seven feet tall. Harry didn't think he'd ever seen anyone so tall before. He was dressed in a black suit with a black shirt and black tie beneath it. His black hair was combed back, and when he smiled, it seemed to make his face grow.

"Where am I?" Harry asked, repeating a

question he had asked Lady Dra Dra.

"You've made it to the end of the game, Harry! You did very well!"

"So . . . what do I get?" Harry asked.

The man smiled widely again, kicking his feet up on his large, oak desk while he sat in his chair. "Well, that's really all up to you," he said.

"How?"

The man sat forward quickly, moving with the speed of a ghost. That grin was still on his face when he leaned over the desk and chuckled. "Harry, my name is B.L. Zebub, and I'm here to offer you a deal you can't possibly turn down!"

Hearing the name, Harry felt as if his entire body was a Popsicle. He'd heard the name before, muttered under the breath of Mayor Kligore. While Harry didn't know the ins and outs of the way We Drive By Night worked, he was pretty sure B.L. Zebub was the head honcho of it all. He was even above Mayor Kligore.

"The game," Harry said. "It was a trick, wasn't it?"

"Well, that depends on how you look at it," B.L. Zebub said. "Didn't you have fun while playing it?"

"For a while," Harry said. "Up until I fell for what seemed like hours. And definitely not the part where those hellhounds were chasing me."

"Hellhounds?" Zebub said. "Oh, you mean Sprinkles and Fluffy? I hope they didn't cause you too much of a scare. They're harmless, really."

"If you say so," Harry said.

B.L. Zebub remained in his chair, never leaving his desk. He studied Harry like a small child might study an insect under a microscope. But the whole time, he wore that menacing smile.

"Fine, I confess," Zebub said. "It was a trick . . . sort of. I developed the MagiKwest app and made sure you got the first download. I figured it was a great way to get you here, into my office."

"Why?" Harry said. He felt fear rising up in him again. He thought the answer to that question was simple; he was pretty sure it involved the mayor and how Harry always seemed to stop his devious plans.

"Because I want to offer you a job," Zebub said.

"You want me to work for you?" Harry asked.

"Of course, Harry. The fact that you got here all by yourself is amazing. I doubt anyone could have figured out those clues, used such magic, and gotten past the horror and temptation I threw your way."

143

"You . . . you did it all on purpose?" Harry asked. "The hounds? Sarah Sinclair?"

"I did," Zebub said, pretending to be ashamed. "But I had to. I needed to make sure you were as good as I always hear you are. And believe me . . . you are. You passed my little test with flying colors, and now I'd like to offer you a job with We Drive By Night."

"No," Harry said, hoping B.L. Zebub could not hear the fear in his voice.

"But you don't even know what the job is."

"I don't need to," Harry said. "You work with the Mayor, and he's done nothing good for Sleepy Hollow. He's a mean and evil man, and I won't work for people he works with."

"Ah, Mayor Kligore," Zebub said. "He's quite loyal but not the brightest ember in the fire, now is he? You know, he complains to me about you all of the time—about how you are always thwarting his plans and outsmarting him and his minions. And that's why I want you on my side, Harry. You and I together . . . we could do some truly great things."

"No," Harry said, without giving it as much as a thought. He was barely aware that he held his wand in his hand, but he really didn't know if it would be useful against such a powerful foe. He really hoped it wouldn't come down to that.

B.L. Zebub finally stood up, kicking his chair back against the wall. In an instant, the office grew much hotter. "Harry, no one says *no* to me. In fact, I'm afraid you don't understand.

There is no option for you. I am no longer *asking*. You either help me or I will destroy you."

Harry saw a flicker of red in the man's eyes that reminded him of the hellhounds. There was something in Zebub's eyes that was evil, but he seemed so pleasant and charming at the same time.

Suddenly, something he'd heard in church popped into his head—something about the Enemy. *The Enemy is not a devil like the ones we imagine with horns and pitchforks,* Reverend Josh had said. *No, he'll come as a charming man—full of beauty and wisdom and promises he has no intention of delivering.*

"Who are you?" Harry asked, already knowing the answer. "Who are you, *really?*"

Zebub smiled brightly. "Oh, I think you know, Harry." Then, with a chuckle that made the room shake and Harry's bones tremble, he added, "I'm your boss."

146

FIREFLIES AND EMPTY SKIES

arry was pretty sure he had never been so scared in all of his life. The seven-foot man was standing less than five feet away from him, and again, Harry's thoughts turned to church—only this time he was thinking of the tale of

David and Goliath.

"This is your last chance, Harry," B.L. Zebub said. "You can give me a *yes* and say that you'll work for me, or you will never see your family and friends again. You'll stay down here with me as my prisoner instead of my employee."

Harry had to think quickly. He would have done anything to have a conversation with Rabbit at that moment; Rabbit seemed to always know what to do in high-pressure situations.

"What *is* the job?" Harry asked, simply trying to buy some time.

Zebub smiled, satisfied. "You'd infiltrate the schools for me," he answered. "You and your Good Mischief Team could work for me. I'd make sure you and your friends get everything you need and everything you could ever want: toys, candy, money, video games, new bikes, the prettiest girls in school . . . whatever you want, Harry."

"And what would we do in the schools?" Harry asked.

"You'd turn them toward . . . well, *bad* mischief. The mayor has done a great job in making Sleepy Hollow dreary and dark in a way that some people don't even realize. But it's the children that shape the future, Harry. And if I can get to *them* . . ."

"Then the town would be yours well into the future," Harry said.

149

"Exactly," Zebub said. "You *are* a bright boy. So what do you say, Harry? A boy your age with the ability to get whatever he wants . . . that would make you *very* powerful."

"If I do this," Harry said, "I'd like something from you first. I need you to prove to me that you're a man of your word."

B.L. Zebub seemed a bit confused by this response, but he recovered quickly. "And what would you like from me?" he asked.

"My wand," Harry said, offering it. "If you're as powerful as you say you are, I want you to make my wand the most powerful one in the world. Can you do that?"

B.L. Zebub laughed again. There was humor in it this time, and that was somehow worse than his menacing chuckle.

"That's child's play, Harry. Why not give me something harder?"

"The wand is all for now," Harry said.

He had a plan in his head as he extended the wand out toward B.L. Zebub. He had no idea if it would work, but it had come to him in the same way the magic words and phrases often jumped into his head.

"Well, as you wish," Zebub said.

He reached out and took the wand, but Harry did not let go. Instead, he took a deep breath and shouted "ABRACADABRA!"

Zebub seemed very confused and then mad. He snatched the wand from Harry and tossed it angrily across the room.

"Were you really trying magic on me?" B.L. Zebub asked. "You foolish boy! The magic of a weak thirteen-year-old baby could not hurt me. And rest assured, I'll have your silly, little head for even trying."

"No, not magic," Harry replied. "Distraction."

151

With that, there was a shout from the closed office door—a scream from Lady Dra Dra's mouth. The office door burst open, and two of the fireflies came in. Only now they were enormous—the size of cars. Their orange glow was nearly blinding now, their wings fluttering in an almost robotic noise.

B.L. Zebub gaped at the fireflies, clearly not expecting such a sight in his office. As he stared, a third huge firefly came in. Then a fourth and a fifth. Behind the huge bugs and the busted office door, Lady Dra Dra was still screaming. She no longer looked pretty, but downright ghoulish in the glow of the fireflies.

Harry took advantage of the distraction and raced to the side of the room where his wand had been thrown. He took it in his hands and wheeled around on B.L. Zebub. Harry was terrified to see that the tall man had extended his arm, and his hand was glowing in a red fireball. Harry searched for any words, any phrase, that might help him, but there was nothing. His head seemed to be empty.

B.L. Zebub let out a yell, and a fireball came bursting from his hand. It struck one of the fireflies, and it instantly shrank back down to its normal size. It then curled up into a burned little U and went to the floor in a pile of ash.

I can't beat him, Harry thought. *I can't win this by fighting. I just have to make it out of here alive.*

The room shook as the rest of the fireflies came in, tearing down the wall. The office was drowned in their strange light as they hovered around Harry, protecting him from B.L. Zebub. Harry flinched as another fireball was tossed from Zebub's hand, killing another of the gigantic fireflies.

Harry had an idea, and as it grew, a series of words came to him, itching in his brain furiously. He shrugged off his book bag and huddled himself around it. He pointed his wand at it and started to speak the words as a third and then a fourth firefly fell into a pile of ash behind him.

With his wand pointed at his book bag, Harry said:

"You are not a bag, you are now a hat!

A magic one, how 'bout that!

I'd pull out a rabbit without making a sound,

but for now, let's pull me out somewhere above ground!"

154

Perhaps it was his utter horror and fear or maybe he hadn't recited the words correctly, but the book bag did not become a magic hat. However, the zipper came undone on its own as if opened up by a ghost. A bright light shone from inside, somewhere near the bottom beyond his now-empty lunch box.

With one final look behind him, Harry saw that B.L. Zebub was burning down another

firefly. There were only two remaining, hovering protectively between him and Harry.

"Thanks, firefly friends," Harry said.

He got on his hands and knees and did his best to crawl inside the book bag. He knew there was no way he could fit, but as soon as his head was inside, the interior of the book bag seemed immense. It was like a big, empty, night sky, waiting for stars to shine. Harry continued to crawl in, and once he was past his shoulders, he felt a tug by an invisible hand. He shot forward into that empty sky.

155

He was dimly aware of a scream behind him. He smiled as he was pulled through the book bag, realizing that it was a shout of frustration from B.L. Zebub.

At the cost of several monstrous fireflies, Harry had managed to escape.

He started falling into the darkness within the bag, and at some point, it was too much. He closed his eyes and fell into the deepest sleep of his life.

156

BACK HOME

arry Moon had been missing for thirty-six hours when the rest of the Good Mischief Team decided that enough was enough. They had to help somehow. They hadn't had any luck with finding clues or rumors at school. It seemed to them like Harry had simply vanished into thin air.

As dusk turned into night, they found themselves on Mayflower Road. It was there that Declan hit his brakes hard. Behind him, Hao and Bailey nearly collided with him.

"What gives, man?" Bailey said.

"Did you guys see that?" Declan asked.

"See what?"

158

"I thought . . . I could have sworn I saw a huge rabbit."

"A rabbit?" Hao asked.

"Yeah. A huge one."

"Guys," Bailey said. "Doesn't Harry have some sort of a rabbit?"

"Yeah, but it's imaginary isn't it?" Declan said.

They fell quiet for a moment, and then they all shrugged at the same time. "Sure," Bailey said. "It may seem weird but . . . let's follow the rabbit."

"A little girl named Alice did that once upon a time," Hao said. "It did not work out so well for her."

"Well, I don't see it now," Declan said.

"Yes, but what way was it headed?" Bailey asked.

"That way," Declan said, pointing to the left.

159

"Then let's go that way," Bailey said.

The three boys took off on their bikes again. For the second time, they passed a location Harry Moon had visited thirty-six hours ago: a house that neighborhood kids sometimes told scary stories about. As they passed by it, a man named Mr. Fang watched from his living room window. It was nearly nightfall, and he'd be able to go out soon enough. But for now, he was happy to just watch as the three boys blazed through the night in search of their friend.

Hao saw him first.

The Good Mischief Team was canvassing the Sleepy Hollow Cemetery, and that was where they found Harry, sleeping soundly behind the grave of Henry David Thoreau. All three boys started cheering as they pedaled over to him. They ditched their bikes and shouted joyfully as they made their way to him.

The commotion woke Harry up with a startled jerk. No sooner had he sat up than he was met with enthusiastic hugs from his friends.

"You scared us all to death!" Declan exclaimed.

"Where have you been? Hao asked.

"How can you be sleeping at a time like this?" Bailey asked.

"Hey guys," Harry said, still clearly half asleep. He looked around the graveyard, and a slow dawning look came over his face.

"What is it, Harry?" Bailey asked. "Are you okay?"

"Oh. My. Gosh," Harry said.

"WHAT?" all three of his friends asked.

"How long . . . have I been gone?"

"Almost two days," Hao said. He sounded like he was on the verge of crying.

161

"I have to get home," Harry said. He got to his feet and started running for the cemetery gates.

"Hold up," Declan said. "Hop on the back of my bike, and I'll give you a ride."

Harry nodded appreciatively and did just that. The four boys left the cemetery on three bikes, the bikes moving perhaps faster than they ever had before. The Good Mischief Team was whole once again, and although the citizens of the town may not have felt it as strongly as the four boys, Sleepy Hollow was also safe and whole again.

Harry was pleased that there was not a big to-do about his return home. A few calls were made to the police, and the chief of police even came by to ask the Moon family some questions. Perhaps the weirdest thing of all, though, was the huge hug Honey Moon gave him. Of course, it was followed by a punch in the arm and her telling him that he'd scared the life out of her, but it was still sweet.

As the night came to an end and Harry Moon settled into his bed, a shape that he had wished for during his time underground leaped up onto his bed.

"Hi, Rabbit," Harry said. "Sorry about all of this. And I'm especially sorry for the way I spoke to you. I don't . . . I don't know what came over me."

"There's no need to apologize to me," Rabbit said. "You have to do certain things to grow. You have to face trials and hardships. And for a boy with your talents, those hardships are often . . . a little strange. And sometimes the things that tempt us can get their claws in a little too deep. I forgive you, Harry."

"Rabbit?"

"Yes, Harry."

"I missed you. After I had sent you away, I wished you were there."

"I know. I could sense it. But your mother . . . I think she needed me more."

"Here?" Harry asked.

Rabbit gave a nod. "While you are strong and have a very bright future ahead of you, those that love you the most have to suffer with you as you grow. Do you understand that?"

"I think so."

Before he could ask Rabbit anything else, there was a knock on his bedroom door. Mary and John Moon poked their heads in. When they did, Rabbit did his usual disappearing act. But Harry knew he was there. Rabbit was always there even when Harry couldn't see him.

His parents sat on the edge of his bed and looked at him with mixed emotions. John Moon reached out and took his son's hand. "You gave us a scare, kiddo."

164

"I know, Dad," he said. "And I'm so sorry."

"We've deleted that game from your phone," Mary Moon said. "And as part of your punishment, you have no cell phone for a month. Is that understood?"

"Yes, Mom."

"Now, are you ready to tell us where you ended up and why you were gone for so long?" Mary asked, her voice on the verge of tears.

"I don't know that I should," Harry said. "I

don't know if I can."

"Is it . . . well, is it about your talents?" John asked.

"Sort of."

"Are you in danger?" he asked.

Harry thought about it for a while. If B.L. Zebub had gone to such great lengths for Harry to come to him, Harry thought that meant that B.L. Zebub could not come directly to Harry. He didn't know why, but that's the way it seemed.

165

"No, I'm not in danger," Harry said.

"We'll discuss your other punishments tomorrow," Mary Moon said. "For now, we're just glad to have you back in our house. But we do want you to know . . . you never have to go through things alone. You will always have family and friends and people that love you."

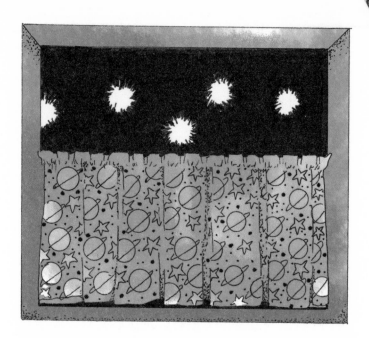

And a rabbit, Harry thought.

"I know," Harry said. "I just let it get way out of control and—"

"Not right now," John said. "Right now, you need to rest."

"But there is one thing we'd like you to do for us before you go to sleep," Mary said.

"Sure, Mom. Anything."

"Let us tuck you in and pray," she said.

And that's exactly what the Moon family did on the night Harry returned home. They huddled around Harry's bed, praying for safety, wisdom, and forgiveness. At the corner of the bed, unseen by the Moon family, a shadow with a lopsided "V" on its head watched over them.

There was one other thing they did not see, lurking by Harry's bedroom window: a small group of fireflies dancing by the glass, shining their pleasant, orange light.

Harry Moon fell asleep. It was a peaceful sleep. At approximately 2:00 a.m. his cell phone buzzed with a new text message. Deep in sleep, Harry did not see the text that said:

> Yes, you won the game, Harry Moon. But don't get yourself too pumped up. The war rages. Consider yourself invited to our party.

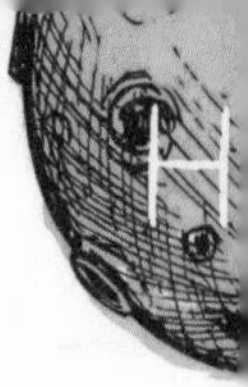
H

169

MARK ANDREW POE

The Adventures of Harry Moon author Mark Andrew Poe never thought about being a children's writer growing up. His dream was to love and care for animals, specifically his friends in the rabbit community.

Along the way, Mark became successful in all sorts of interesting careers. He entered the print and publishing world as a young man and his company did really, really well.

Mark became a popular and nationally

sought-after health care advocate for the care and well-being of rabbits.

Years ago, Mark came up with the idea of a story about a young man with a special connection to a world of magic, all revealed through a remarkable rabbit friend. Mark worked on his idea for several years before building a collaborative creative team to help bring his idea to life. And Harry Moon was born.

In 2014, Mark began a multi-book print series project intended to launch *The Adventures of Harry Moon* into the youth marketplace as a hero defined by a love for a magic where love and 'DO NO EVIL' live. Today, Mark continues to work on the many stories of Harry Moon. He lives in suburban Chicago with his wife and his 25 rabbits.

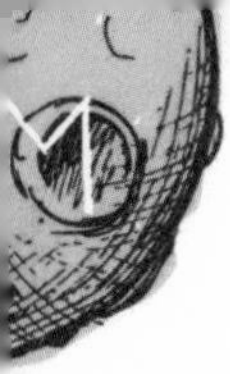

172

BE SURE TO READ THE CONTINUING AND
AMAZING ADVENTURES OF HARRY MOON

THE
AMAZING
Adventures Of

HARRY MOON

Wand - Paper - Scissors

Inspired by true events   Mark Andrew Poe

HARRY MOON is up to his eyeballs in magic in the small town of Sleepy Hollow. His arch enemy, Titus Kligore, has eyes on winning the Annual Scary Talent Show. Harry has a tough job ahead if he is going to steal the crown. He takes a chance on a magical rabbit who introduces him to the deep magic. Harry decides the best way forward is to DO NO EVIL— and the struggle to defeat Titus while winning the affection of the love of his life goes epic.

EVERYONE IS TALKING ABOUT THE ADVENTURES OF HARRY MOON

"After making successful Disney movies like ALADDIN and LITTLE MERMAID, I could never figure out where the magic came from. Now I know. Harry Moon had it all along."

David Kirkpatrick
Former Production Chief, Walt Disney Studios

"This may well be one of the most important kid's series in a long time."

- Paul Lewis,
Founder,
Family University
Foundation

"Come on. His name is Harry Moon. How do I not read this?"

- Declan Black
Kid, age 13

"A great coming-of-age book with life principals. Harry Moon is better than Goosebumps and Wimpy Kid. Who'da thunk it?

- Michelle Borquez
Author and Mom

THE
AMAZING
ADVENTURES OF
HARRY MOON

TIME MACHINE

Inspired by true events   Mark Andrew Poe

The irrepressible magician of Sleepy Hollow, Harry Moon, sets about to speed up time. Overnight, through some very questionable magic, Harry wishes himself into becoming the high school senior of his dreams. Little did he know that by unleashing time, Harry Moon would come face-to-face with the monster of his worst nightmare. Will Harry find his way home from this supernatural mess?

EVERYONE IS TALKING *ABOUT* THE ADVENTURES OF HARRY MOON

"Friendship, forgiveness and adventure – Harry Moon will entertain kids and parents alike. My children will have every book in this series on their bookshelf as my gift to them!"
– Regina Jennings
Author and Mom

"Magical and stupendously inspirational, Harry Moon is a hero for the 21st century tween. I wish I had Harry at DISNEY!"
David Kirkpatrick
Former Production Chief, Walt Disney Studios

I love my grandchildren and I love Harry Moon. I can't wait to introduce the kids to someone their own age who values life like I do. I hope Harry Moon never ends.
– Scott Hanson
Executive Director, Serve West Dallas and grandpa

I can't wait for my next book. Where is the Harry Moon video game?
– Jackson Maison
Kid - age 12

The AMAZING Adventures Of

HARRY MOON

Halloween Nightmares

Inspired by true events   Mark Andrew Poe

While other kids are out trick-or-treating, eighth-grade magician Harry Moon is flying on a magic cloak named Impenetrable. Harry and Rabbit speed past severed hands, boiling cauldrons and graveyard witching rituals on their way to unravel a decade old curse at the annual Sleepy Hollow Halloween Bonfire. The sinister Mayor Kligore and Oink are in for the fight of their lives.

EVERYONE IS TALKING ABOUT THE ADVENTURES OF HARRY MOON

"When a character like Harry Moon comes along, you see how important a great story can be to a kid growing up."

- Susan Dawson,
Middle School Teacher

"Harry Moon is one wildly magical ride. After making successful films like ALADDIN and LITTLE MERMAID, I wondered where the next hero was coming from. Harry Moon has arrived!"

David Kirkpatrick
Former Production Chief, Walt Disney Studios

"A hero with guts who champions truth in the face of great danger. I wish I was thirteen again! If you work with kids, pay attention to Harry Moon."

- Ryan Frank, a Dad and
President, KidzMatter

"This is a book I WANT to read."

- Bailey Black
13-Year Old Kid

$14.99
ISBN 978-1-943785-02-5

51499>

THE
AMAZING
Adventures Of

HARRY MOON

The Scary Smart House

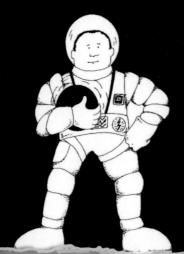

Inspired by true events   Mark Andrew Poe

When Harry's sister wins a national essay contest in technology, the whole Moon family is treated to a dream weekend in the ultimate, fully loaded, smart house designed by Marvel Modbot, the Walt Disney of the 21st century. It's an incredible blast, with driverless cars and a virtual reality world. That is, until evil thinking invades the smart technology running the smart house, turning that dream tech weekend into an nightmare! The Moons look to Harry and Rabbit to stop the evil before its too late.

EVERYONE IS TALKING ABOUT THE ADVENTURES OF HARRY MOON

"The Moon family's smart house takes on a bone-tingling dimension when the technology that runs it appears haunted. Say hello to SECOS –a scary Smart Evil Central Operating System!" –David Kirkpatrick, Former Production Chief, Walt Disney Studios

I'm a grandpa and Harry Moon is a throw-back to the good old days when kids took on wrong and wrestled it to the ground. My grandkids are getting every book."

- Mark Janes, English and Drama Teacher, Grandfather

"If I was stranded on a desert island, I would want a mat, a pillow, a Harry Moon book and a hatchet"
- Charley, KID, age 11

"I pride myself on never making a bad shot. I focus on perfect form and being rock steady. Like me, Harry Moon delivers under pressure. This kid's my hero."

- Jim Burnworth, Extreme Archer, The Outdoor Channel

THE
AMAZING
Adventures Of

HARRY MOON

HAUNTED PIZZA

Inspired by true events   Mark Andrew Poe

The new Pizza Slice is doing booming business, but the kids in Sleepy Hollow Middle School are transforming into strange creatures the more they eat of the haunted cheesy delicacy. Even the Good Mischief Team are falling under the spell of the new haunted pizza slices, putting Harry and his magic Rabbit on the scent to the truth behind the peperoni mystery.

EVERYONE IS TALKING ABOUT THE ADVENTURES OF HARRY MOON

"The Moon family's smart house takes on a bone-tingling dimension when the technology that runs it appears haunted. Say hello to SECOS -a scary Smart Evil Central Operating System!" –David Kirkpatrick, Former Production Chief, Walt Disney Studios

In a grandpa and Harry Moon is a throw-back to the good old days when kids took on wrong and wrestled it to the ground. My grandkids are getting every book."

- Mark Janes, English and Drama Teacher, Grandfather

"If I was stranded on a desert island, I would want a mat, a pillow, a Harry Moon book and a hatchet"
- Charley, KID, age 11

"I pride myself on never making a bad shot. I focus on perfect form and being rock steady. Like me, Harry Moon delivers under pressure. This kid's my hero."
- Jim Burnworth, Extreme Archer, The Outdoor Channel

$14.99 US / $22.50 CAN
ISBN 978-1-943785-38-4

THE ENCHANTED WORLD OF HONEY MOON

MOUNTAIN MAYHEM

Suzanne Brooks Kuhn

Created by Mark Andrew Poe

Hit the trail girls! It's on to the Appalachian Trail. Honey and the Spooky Scouts set off on a mountain trek to earn their final Mummy Mates patch. But an inept troop leader, a flash flood and a campfire catastrophe threaten to keep them from reaching the Sleepy Hollow finish line in time. When all seems lost, Honey Moon takes charge and nothing will stop her from that final patch!

"Honey is a bit of magical beauty...adventure and brains rolled into one."
David Kirkpatrick, Former Production Chief, Walt Disney Studios

"Magic, mystery and a little mayhem. Three things that make a story great. Honey Moon is a great story."
-- Dawn Moore
Life Coach and Educator

"A wonderful experience for girls looking for a new hero. I think her name is Honey Moon." - Nancy Dimes, Teacher & Mom

"I absolutely cannot wait to begin my next adventure with Honey Moon. I love her" - Carly Wujcik, Kid, age 11

"Charm, wit and even a bit of mystery. Honey Moon is a terrific piece of writing that will keep kids asking for more."
--Priscilla Strapp, Writer, Foster Mom

$14.99 US / $22.50 CAN

9 781943 785186

90000>

THE ENCHANTED WORLD OF

HONEY MOON

Shades and Shenanigans

Suzanne Brooks Kuhn   Created by Mark Andrew Poe

When Honey comes face-to-face with
Clarice Kligore and her Royal Shades
she knows something must be done to
keep this not very nice club from
taking over Sleepy Hollow Elementary.
Honey sets out to beat them at their
own game by forming her own club,
The Queen Bees. Instead of chasing the
Shades off the playground for good,
Honey learns that being the Queen Bee
is more about the honey than the sting.

"Honey goes where she is needed . . . and everyone needs Honey Moon!"
— David Kirkpatrick, Former Production Chief, Walt Disney Studios

"I wish Honey Moon had been written when
my girls were young. She would have charmed
her way into their hearts."
- Nora Wolfe, Mother of Two

"Heart, humor, age-
appropriate puppy love
and wisdom. Honey's
not perfect but she is
striving to be a good,
strong kid."
— Anne Brighen
Elementary School Teacher

"My favorite character of
all time. I love Honey."
- Elise Rogers, Age 9

"I am a grandmother. I knew ahead of time that these books were
aimed at younger readers but I could not resist and thank goodness
for that! A great kid's book!"
--Carri Zimmerman, Grandmother of Twelve

$14.99
ISBN 978-1-943785-16-2
51499>

9 781943 785162

The
ENCHANTED
WORLD OF
HONEY
MOON

NOT YOUR VALENTINE

Regina Jennings   Created by Mark Andrew Poe

A Sleepy Hollow Valentine's Day dance with a boy! NO WAY, NO HOW is Honey Moon going to a scary sweetheart dance with that Noah kid. But, after being forced to dance together in PE class, word gets around that Honey likes Noah. Now, she has no choice but to stop Valentine's Day in its tracks. Things never go as planned and Honey winds up with the surprise of her Sleepy Hollow life.

"Honey is a breakout wonder... What a pint-sized powerhouse!"
- David Kirkpatrick, Former Production Chief, Walt Disney Studios

"A dance, a boy and Honey Moon - every girl wants to know how this story will end up."
- Deby Less, Mom and Teacher

"What better way to send a daughter off to sleep than knowing she can conquer any problem by doing the right thing."
- Jean Zyskowski Mom and Office Manager

"I love to read and Honey Moon is my favorite of all!"
- Lilah Black, KID age 8

"Makes me want to have daughters again so they could grow up with Honey Moon. Strong and vulnerable heroines make raising healthy children even more exciting.
--Suzanne Kuhn, Best-selling Author Coach

$14.99
ISBN 978-1-943785-08-7
51499>

9 781943 785087

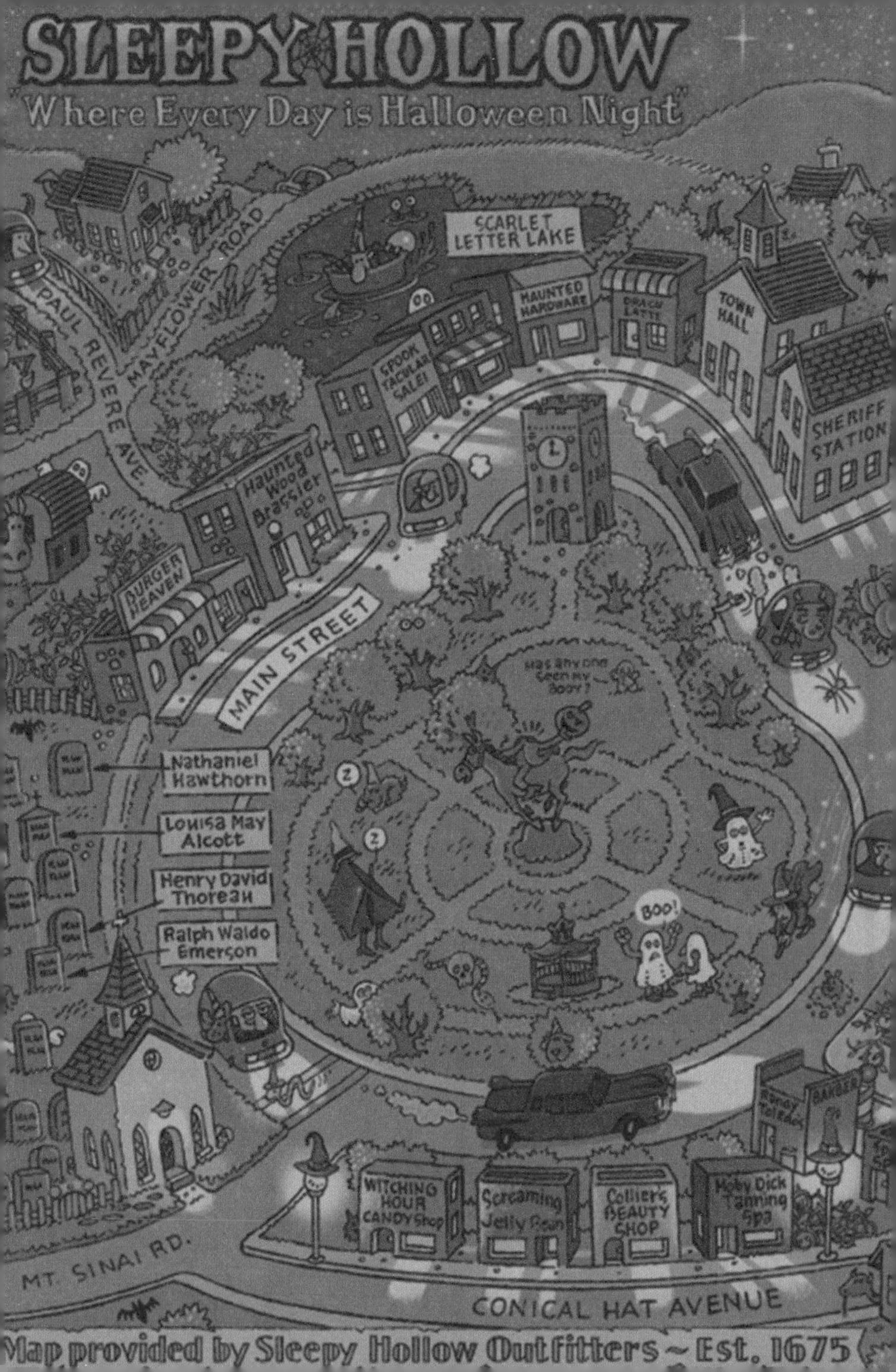
SLEEPY HOLLOW
"Where Every Day is Halloween Night"
SCARLET LETTER LAKE
MAYFLOWER ROAD
PAUL REVERE AVE.
HAUNTED HARDWARE
TOWN HALL
SHERIFF STATION
SPOOK TACULAR SALE!
Haunted Wood Brassier
BURGER HEAVEN
MAIN STREET
Has anyone seen my Body?
BOO!
Nathaniel Hawthorn
Louisa May Alcott
Henry David Thoreau
Ralph Waldo Emerson
WITCHING HOUR CANDY Shop
Screaming Jelly Bean
Collier's BEAUTY SHOP
Moby Dick Tanning Spa
BARBER
MT. SINAI RD.
CONICAL HAT AVENUE
Map provided by Sleepy Hollow Outfitters ~ Est. 1675